Semiotics of Peasants in Transition

Sound and Meaning

The Roman Jakobson Series

in Linguistics and Poetics

C. H. van Schooneveld,

Series Editor

Irene Portis-Winner

✿ Semiotics of Peasants in Transition

Slovene Villagers and

Their Ethnic Relatives

in America

Duke University Press   Durham and London   2002

© 2002 Duke University Press

All rights reserved

Printed in the United States of America

on acid-free paper ∞

Designed by C. H. Westmoreland

Typeset in Minion by Keystone Typesetting, Inc.

Library of Congress Cataloging-in-Publication

Data appear on the last printed page of

this book.

To Benjamin and Kyla with love

Contents

Acknowledgments ix

I The Dynamics of a Dialogic Relation between a Peasant
Village and Its Ethnic Counterpart: *A Semiotic Approach*

Prologue: "The Strange Intruder" (from Peirce): *A Peasant Village
and Its Many Others* 3

1. A Glance at the Village and Its Sister Ethnic Communities
in Cleveland and Hibbing 11

II Theoretical Issues and Terminology:
From the Outer to the Inner Point of View

2. Nationalism, Ethnic Identity, Transnationalism: *Issues of
Terminology* 31

3. Can We Find the Inner Point of View? *Interpretative Anthropology,
Performance Anthropology* 43

4. Semiotics of Culture 50

III The Village and the Slovene Communities in Cleveland and
Hibbing: *A Historical Perspective*

5. Žerovnica: *Its Past and the Question of the Future* 77

6. The Story of the Ethnic Community in Cleveland 106

IV Semiotic Portraits

7. Semiotic Portraits in Cultural Context 127

8. Concluding Remarks 152

Notes 157
Selected Bibliography 161
Index 181

Acknowledgments

I wish to thank the following foundations and individuals who supported this study: the International Research and Exchanges Committee (IREX) in 1992 provided a grant in aid for travel to Žerovnica, and in 1995 it supported my travel to the Czech Republic to present some of my findings at a conference on Jakobson. The Joint Committee on Eastern Europe of the American Council of Learned Societies provided grants in 1973 for work in Žerovnica, in 1975–76 for work among Žerovnicans in Cleveland and Minnesota, and in 1977 for the research and writing of a position paper on the semiotics of culture. A USIA grant provided funds for presenting some of my theoretical work at the Masaryk University in Brno, Czech Republic; and a grant from the Immigration History Archives of the University of Minnesota provided a grant for the use of their archival materials, opening these holdings to me most generously. All these grants are gratefully acknowledged. My last stay in Slovenia in 1995 was partly financed by the Scientific Research Center (*Znanstveni in raziskovalni center*) of the Slovene Academy of Sciences and the Arts (*SAZU*). Its Director, Dr. Oto Luthar, invited me to present a paper on my project at the Slovene Academy of Sciences and Arts.

In Žerovnica and its sister village Grahovo, many helped. We must let a listing of a few suffice. In 1964–65 the late Marija (Micka) Mertelj provided space in her house in Grahovo for our family, my husband and two (then) teenage daughters. And her son Marijan, now deceased, and his wife, Marija, and their daughter, Meta Polovič, continued this hospitality. In Žerovnica proper, my heartfelt thanks go out to the family of the late Matija and Marija Rok. Matija Rok had been the village headman of Žerovnica until the Communist administration deprived the village of its autonomy. He still held much of the village documentation such as maps and deeds in his possession, and he was a welcome fount of information and wisdom. Both Matija and Marija Rok became close friends, and their hospitality knew no bounds. The same can be said of the next generation of the family, the Roks' daughter Marija, now deceased, her husband Anton (Tone) Primožič, and their daughters, Marija and Antonia (Tončka), both of whose births and first birthdays we celebrated in Žerovnica in the 1960s. Much help was also received from the various priests in the Grahovo parish that includes Žerovnica. Father Metod Lampe provided village records and allowed my assistant access to the archives. One of his predecessors supplied us with initial archival material, thus enabling us to enter the village with at least a rudimentary knowledge of its structure. When we returned in the 1970s, we heard that he had been jailed, and to this day we are afraid that this was caused by our frequent visits to his parish office. He is now a priest in Maribor. My greatest debt in the village goes to Meta Polovič, Marijan and Marija Mertelj's daughter, who was born during our stay in the Merteljs' house in Grahovo in the 1960s. Meta is now a teacher in the Grahovo primary school that also serves Žerovnica. She was my research assistant in the nineties and provided much helpful information and documentation. To her a great *Najlepša hvala in topel objem!*

I also wish to thank the following scholars. First of all, I am grateful to the late Roman Jakobson from whom I learned much through his lectures, writings, and many conversations during long walks on Ossabaw Island and in his and our houses in Cambridge and Vermont. It was his interest in semiotics and in Peirce that proved particularly helpful to me. I wish to thank the late Conrad Arensberg for his general comments and for his help with the question of the joint family and the twelve-family origin myth. I also wish to thank the late Eric Wolf for his valuable comments on my article about transnationals and the human sign, which forms the basis of a large part of chapter 2, and for his explorations into the semiotics of power about which we corresponded. My special gratitude goes to Gérard Deledalle for his invaluable communications concerning Peirce and his sign types. I learned much from him. Rado Lenček, founder and past president of the Slovene Society in the United States, gave unfailing support and encouragement for my Slovene research and provided many opportunities for presenting papers on its progress. I am grateful for his helpful comments on modern Slovenia.

I am greatly indebted to Cornelis van Schooneveld for his unfailing support of this project. My Slovene friends, Academician Franc Jakopin and his wife Gitica in Ljubljana, first steered me to Žerovnica. Jakopin's father had grown up in Žerovnica, and Franc had living relatives there. Our introduction to his relatives in Grahovo (the Merteljs) gave us a special and unusual entry into the village and provided us with a domicile. I am grateful to him for inviting me to present some of my findings about Žerovnica and

Cleveland to the Scientific Research Center of the Slovene Academy of Arts and Sciences in May 1995. Professor Rudolph Vecoli at the University of Minnesota, and at the time of my work in Minneapolis the director of the University's Immigration History Research Center, was of great help to me. And also Jurij Fikfak (Slovene Academy of Sciences), who read this manuscript in its early stage and provided valuable suggestions. I am indebted to Michael Herzfeld (Anthropology, Harvard), who read this manuscript in various stages, and gave valuable suggestions from which I greatly benefited. Finally, I extend my thanks to those editors at Duke University Press whose meticulous reading was of great value.

Among Cleveland Slovenes, I am indebted to Josephine Turkman and her late husband Andrew, who were our hosts in their Cleveland house during an extended research stay in 1976. Mrs. Turkman was the founder and musical director of the Slovene choral society Zarja. Both Turkmans helped us in gaining entry to the Cleveland Slovene environment. Great thanks are also due to Rudolph Susel (Šušelj), the editor of the Cleveland Slovene newspaper *Ameriška domovina* (American Homeland), for many useful and instructive discussions and for his coeditorship of one of my books touching on the Cleveland Slovenes. I also received invaluable help from Allen Urbanič who researched archival records for me in Cleveland.

My thanks also go to Dr. Oto Luthar, Director of the Scientific Research Center of the Slovene Academy of Sciences and the Arts, who provided financial support for our last stay in Slovenia in 1995 and who invited me to present a discussion of my project as a lecture in his center. Professor Jerzy Pelc at the University of Warsaw, Poland, and past President of the International Association of Semiotic Studies, kindly invited me to present some of my findings to the Polish Semiotic Society in 1990. I am grateful for this and for many stimulating discussions with him.

Last but not least, I wish to thank my husband, Thomas G. Winner, a Slavist, who participated with me in all the fieldwork, gave me many helpful comments, and read every chapter of this book. In this sense, the study was a joint enterprise, and the double point of view gained was invaluable.

I

The Dynamics of a Dialogic

Relation between a Peasant Village

and Its Ethnic Counterpart:

A Semiotic Approach

"The Strange Intruder" (From Peirce):
A Peasant Village and Its Many Others

This book is a semiotic study of the intercommunication, verbal and non-verbal, implicit and explicit, within and between two communities. The first is a traditional and ancient Slovene village, Žerovnica, situated in the Notranjsko region of Slovenia, while the second emerged as a result of the diaspora beginning in the 1890s when severe poverty required households in Žerovnica and other Slovene villages to send at least one family member to Cleveland, Ohio, thereby founding a Slovene-American ethnic community. While Cleveland was the location of choice, some migrants established themselves in the small town of Hibbing, Minnesota.

The interpretation of the transnational and ethnic quality that bound these two communities presents a key concern for this study. For not only did the overseas group mold many of its practices and institutions after traditions remembered from the mother villages; the mind-set of the inhabitants of Žerovnica and other comparable villages also forever changed as a result of the intensive and pervasive identification with Cleveland. Transnationalism, the participation in and identification with two cultures, one native and one "other," has been, of course, a significant concomitant of contemporary globalization, and there are few communities left today that are isolated or closed in the traditional anthropological sense. Moreover, the ethnic phenomenon, the reaction to or participation in an impinging alien group, has essentially been with us since the dawn of culture, although it has often been overlooked or not sufficiently stressed.

The flow of Slovene migrants to the United States, motivated mainly by economic concerns, began during the crises of the 1880s and continued, albeit at a somewhat slower rate after 1914 due to restrictive U.S. immigration quotas, until World War II. During the communist rule in Yugoslavia, emigration from the Yugoslav republics essentially halted, but a new wave of migrants composed primarily of Slovenes who emigrated from German or Austrian displaced persons' (DP) camps because of their opposition to communist rule. It is the long and intense dialogue between the Slovene villagers and the early ethnic communities in Cleveland and outlying areas, as well as in Hibbing, Minnesota, that is the focus of this study.

I gathered the data for this book during five fieldwork stays in Žerovnica and nearby villages from 1964 through 1995, as well as during four research stays in Cleveland and Hibbing from 1974 through 1995. My first book on the village, *Žerovnica: A Slovenian Village* (1971) was a holistic sociostructural analysis of this traditional peasant village and was cast in historical as well as spatial context, that is within the framework of the village's relations with the outside world.

The present book consists of four main sections. Part 1 includes this prologue that introduces the study's background and presents a brief look at the most relevant semiotically oriented scholars. It also includes chapter 1 that presents an introductory glance at the village and the Slovene groups in Cleveland and Hibbing. Part 2 (chapters 2 and 3) concentrates on theoretical positions, reviews questions of terminology in relation to ethnicity and identity, and asks how we can find the inner point of view. A significant effort was Geertz's "From the Native Point of View: On the Nature of Anthropological Understanding" (1983b, 55–70); but it lacked the richness and complexity of the position taken by the semioticians discussed in this study. The whole issue of the interpenetration of the anthropologist's often ethnocentric position, conscious or not, and values and outlooks of the group studied has become a much discussed problem. Part 3, composed only of one chapter (chapter 4), takes up in greater detail the concepts of semiotically oriented scholars that are relevant to this study of transnationals, communication, and meaning. Part 4 consists of three chapters (chapters 5, 6, and 7), all of which discuss the ethnography of the two communities within a semiotic framework. In chapter 5, concerning Žerovnica, the aim is to explore local documented history, memory, myths, rituals, traditional and everyday activities, as well as major contemporary changes from the complexities of the inner point of view as well as the official or other points of view. Chapter 6 relates the story of the U.S. immigrants from their point of view, including their memories of the home village. Chapter 7 sketches the contrasting attitudes of youth and elders both in Žerovnica and in Cleveland. My portrayal of what I call extended human signs, the "man-sign" in Peirce's terminology, comprises the majority of this chapter. Such signs, composed of interlinked individuals of more than one generation, conjoin the two communities in paradigmatic and syntagmatic interrelations.

How did I come to the semiotic theories that make up the framework for the present study? First of all, the data collected in Žerovnica during the original fieldwork in 1964–65 seemed to me to call for a study of ways of signaling and communicating aspects of ethnic discourse and self-evaluation. The evidence of relations to Cleveland was prominently displayed everywhere in the village houses. Calendar pictures, gifts, and letters told tales of continual contact with overseas relatives. Without the remittances sent home by these migrants, the villagers in fact believed, Žerovnica could not have survived the depressions of the 1890s and 1930s. As my work progressed in 1964–65, it became increasingly clear to me that my local study presented only a partial picture since Cleveland was in the hearts, minds, and worldview of all villagers. Their first question to us was almost always, "Do you know Cleveland?" ("*Ali poznata Kleveland?*"). Thus I resolved to make a second study encompassing the relations of the Slovene ethnic community in the United States with the home village. Second, since completing my 1971 study, my dominant interests have shifted to questions of meaning, communication, and transnationalism, and during the past decades I have given considerable thought to semiotic theories of meaning and communication of information in culture. I believe that they provide many creative and fruitful tools in analyzing the ethnological materials gathered and allow me to rethink the earlier findings in my first study of Žerovnica.

A Bird's-Eye View of the Evolving Theories
of the Semiotics of Culture

I consider semiotics and semiotics of culture overall perspectives rather than disciplines. Interest in signs and communication has a long history traceable to the writings of the Stoics and St. Augustine, to Kant's emphasis on the perceiving and thinking mind, Locke's concept of the sign, and Vico's hypothesis that man knows the world only imperfectly since he knows only what he can do or make. For Vico, natural language is simply an adequate means of communication, not a precise instrument, and is, in fact, a reflection of a whole cultural way of life. Vico's anti-Cartesianism and his view that understanding a culture is like understanding a language since ways of life are embedded in ways of speaking, make him a forerunner of semiotics of culture.[1] Saussure, the creator of structural linguistics, was the first to call for the study of culture as a system of signs.

The primary semiotically oriented thinkers on whom I draw are Charles Sanders Peirce (1849–1914), Roman Jakobson (1896–1982), Jan Mukařovský (1891–1975), Petr Bogatyrev (1893–1970), Mikhail Bakhtin (1895–1975), Yury Lotman (1922–93), Boris Uspensky, and Vjačeslav Ivanov. While Peirce's writings spanned the late nineteenth and early twentieth centuries and Bakhtin began writing in the 1920s, the publication of their revolutionary studies was generally delayed until after their respective deaths, and it is only comparatively recently that they have begun to receive the attention they deserve. Peirce's definition of the sign is still the classic one, and it is employed in this study:

> A sign or representation is something which stands for somebody for something in some respect or capacity. It addresses somebody, that is creates in the mind of that person an equivalent, or perhaps more developed, sign. That sign which it creates I call *the interpretant* of the first sign. That sign stands for it for something, its *object.* It stands for the object not in all respects but in reference to a sort of idea (CP 2.228). And Nothing is a sign unless it is interpreted as a sign. (CP 2.308)[2]

Bakhtin's scrutiny of medieval carnival behavior and the novel, particularly those of Dostoyevsky and Rabelais, informed his concepts of dialogue, double-voiced discourse, heteroglossia, carnival reversals, the grotesque, humor, and his emphasis on unofficial culture. His denial of any single point of view essentially destroyed the concept of the omniscient authorial voice.

Saussure, in his *Course in General Linguistics,* posthumously published in French from student lecture notes in 1917, held that all manifestations of both verbal and nonverbal behavior are aspects of sign systems, although he saw verbal messages as the primary ones, and called for an investigation of all cultural sign systems (Saussure 1966, 16). This call was taken up in the work of the Prague School and later, in the 1970s, by the Moscow-Tartu School, both of which rejected Saussure's logocentrism, his monofunctional interpretation of *langue* and its strict separation from *parole*, as well as his rigid dichotomy of synchrony and diachrony. The Prague Linguistic Circle, formed in 1926, and its members, particularly Roman Jakobson and Jan Mukařovský, introduced the concept of the multifunctional and polysemic message, rejected the synchrony/diachrony dichotomy, refused to separate linguistics and poetics, and advocated the omnipresent nature of the aesthetic function.

Under the leadership of Yury M. Lotman of the University of Tartu in Estonia, the Moscow-Tartu School introduced the *semiotics of culture*, as a concept and investigated the interrelated sign systems in culture, resulting in the notion of *culture text* ("Theses" 1973) as the unit in culture that is meaningful. In their 1973 "Theses," the Moscow-Tartu scholars attempted to integrate the various areas of semiotics pertaining to humans under a single overarching concept, later called by Lotman the *semiosphere*.

In summary, semiotics of culture focuses on signs and their texts in all possible modes. From this perspective, the semiotic endeavor as applied to culture is always wedded to an open and exploratory approach that is demonstrably heuristic, suggesting further paths of research. In this study I will concentrate on the *semiotics of ethnic culture texts*. And the specific actors I consider in this study are saturated with *transnational* energies. But how, and in what sense, are culture texts ethnic? From a semiotic perspective they are so understood if they are interpreted by any of the interlocutors as referring or contributing to information about any of the latter's valued characteristics (as contrasted to some *other* with different or opposing traits). Indeed, the observing anthropologist may interpret ethnic culture texts as having a commenting role or hovering on a metalevel that answers the question "who am I as opposed to them?," marking self-identity and self-evaluation.

The issue of ethnicity becomes more complex for American Slovenes of the younger generation. Are the differences, Slovene versus American, always valorized or are they rejected? Is the phenomenon of searching for one's roots, apparent among some of the youth today, partially a reaction to the melting pot society? Membership in ethnic groups is changeable and unfixed, and hence ethnic culture cannot be reduced in any permanent sense to a particular group or a particular bounded space. Whether a culture text should be considered an ethnic text thus depends on the point of view of the actors, the outlook of the observer, or both.

The Modern Crisis of Representation

Whereas the values of the recent past held that differences between groups in contact may contribute, at least in part, to a richer and more diverse culture and to cooperative activities, the present era is flooded with conflict and hostility between ethnic groups. The power of official maps and imposed geographical boundaries have been eroded. Slovenia has been fortunate to escape the brunt of ethnic conflict and violence in the former Yugoslavia, and of course the Slovene-American community partakes of such an advantage. Yet such massive upheavals as the ones taking place in Eastern Europe penetrate all aspects of the ethnographic dialogue. Accordingly, the task of selecting emphases and materials and bringing to light the inner point of view includes a new dimension. As Frederick Barth has pointed out, urging the study of culture as process rather than as a closed system,

> there is a surfeit of cultural materials and ideational possibilities available from which to construct reality. The anthropologist has no basis for assuming that all these materials are contained in one complete, logically compelling package or structure. (1993, 4–5)

Barth implies that oversimplification and reduction can only lead to questionable answers and therefore calls for the uncovering of interconnections of ideas and differences.

This undertaking is made exponentially more complex by current cultural, political, and economic clashes. Do the ideals and principles of Enlightenment humanism and rationalism still universally apply today? Is there still a positive and fruitful role for ethnic differences in the celebration of creativity and diversity? The failure of a positivist program to illuminate meanings and interrelationships not only of the outer view but also of the inner perspective proves a further obstacle. Additionally, the omniscient, objective, authorial, or scholarly voice is now seen as a distortion or a contributing factor to understanding that must be accounted for. Can we see ethnography as a kind of story or narration, a cooperative endeavor between informant and ethnologist, a plurivocal interchange that, if so interpreted, employs, consciously or not, many kinds of tropes but also sees anthropology as part of the world of science and the arts? We may wonder about the quality of warnings proclaimed by Eugene Hammel (1994), Robert Hayden (1993), and Robert Gary Minnich (1993) when they asked whether the disasters in the former Yugoslavia may spell the end of anthropology as we know it.

Hammel writes:

> Our adherence to antiracist principles enunciated by Boas and later by Mead and Kluckhohn and others . . . may be on a collision course with the re-emergence of ethnicity (sometimes symbolized as religion) as the backbone of political and social organization. . . . The problem is thus bigger than Yugoslavia. But it is also bigger than the convenient use of ethnic particularism as a replacement for universalistic rationality. . . . It raises some fundamental problems for us as anthropologists, especially in the area of human rights. . . . It means that you can be a citizen based on where you live rather than on where you came from. . . . Cultural relativism, in my view, is a worthless concept when the issues are those of life and death, of personal degradation, of all those values that are at the core of our own concepts of civil and human rights. What if Boas was wrong? (1994, 1–3)

This overturning of past values following the demise of a multiethnic Yugoslavia also causes Minnich to despair. Describing Slovenia's successful bid for independence, he writes that when the presidency of Yugoslavia was in the hands of advocates for a "Greater Serbia," Slovenia took steps toward independence—and was the only republic to escape prolonged warfare. As he notes, the history of Yugoslavia—its initial consolidation—was a "shotgun wedding" and that in the interwar period Yugoslavia failed to establish a democratic and equitable division of power (1993, 78–79). The nineteenth-century national awakening impeded by World War I and the interests of the great powers created the chaotic circumstances in which the Balkan states were arbitrarily construed with political frontiers that did not "satisfy their respective peoples' modern aspirations for self-determination." As Minnich holds, "self-determination can be a positive factor for state making . . . only if founded on a rule of law and on the creation of a trans-ethnic political administration and judicial system" as opposed to the "heavy-handed role of totalitarian leaders" (1993, 79).

Here we are faced with a double challenge. First, we need to search for analytical tools and theories that can help in the difficult task of saving or giving rebirth to basic human values. These values should allow rationalism, human rights, and diversity to flourish in combination with peaceful self-determination. They should rest on underlying universals such as bio-psychological principles and concepts of space-time in which ethnicity is not exploited as a rationalization for xenophobic nationalism or power plays by nations weak and strong, and where history is not reduced to traces. Second, we are equally challenged to question the historical and ideological reasons for our present dilemma.

Chapter One

A Glance at the Village and Its Sister
Ethnic Communities in Cleveland and Hibbing

Early Impressions of the Village:
Žerovnica from the Sixties to the Present

Žerovnica is located in the Notranjsko area in the administrative district (*občina*) of Cerknica in southwestern Slovenia. Its land abuts the Cerknica basin (*Cerkniško polje*) where the periodically disappearing karstic Cerknica lake (*Cerkniško jezero;* the phenomenon is called *presihajoče jezerox*) an extremely important *dramatis persona* in village lore is located. The Cerknica area is bordered by mountains to the northeast and southwest.

In the 1960s, when we (my husband, our two teenage daughters, Ellen and Lucy, and I) first stayed in the village, Slovene peasant villages appeared relatively isolated, and Žerovnica was no exception despite the proximity of the Brest ("Elm") furniture factories and the impinging Marof cooperative farm (*zadruga*), both visible as we drove toward Žerovnica.

The outside observer, standing at a distance from the village, perceives what appears to be a harmoniously bounded whole. Yet I soon learned about a long tradition of emigration to the United States that began in the 1880s and was believed necessary for the survival of the village. In spite of appearances, the village had porous boundaries, and the distance did not break the ties between migrants and the villagers back home. However, endogamy or marriage to partners in neighboring villages was common and preferred, and the history of the village supports the conclusion that much of the feudal economic structure and value system survived in spite of the long period of communist domination. A look at a relief model of Žerovnica exhibited at the Ljubljana Geographic Institute, the legend of which describes the village as "a typical road village on the southeast side of the [Cerknica] basin," also supports such a perspective. The caption locates Žerovnica in one of the most typical traditional Slovenian regions,

A map of Slovenia (above) and Cerknica občina where Žerovnica is located.

Žerovnica, a typical road village

an area in which land is still divided into the same strips as during the Middle Ages. The town lies in a large triangular area, with the Cerknica basin at its center. The caption continues: there are "narrow, impossibly divided strips that compose clearly defined land complexes. . . . In each complex the most significant families each have one piece."

I gained my first perception of the village in the summer of 1964 as my family and I drove our Volkswagen minivan along a straight, dusty, then unpaved road leading south in the Cerknica plain. Two striking landmarks come to view as the traveler approaches the village from the north. The first is the partisan monument, a large, rough-hewn stone placed at the entrance of the village, standing next to a wooden bridge over the Žerovniščenia stream near the building of the fire brigade (*gasilski dom*) and the *balina* field.[1] On the monument the names of fallen heroes, the partisan fighters against the Germans and Italians, are inscribed. The second dramatic landmark, at the far southern end of the village on a sizable hill occupying the highest ground, is the village church crowned by its red (now painted green) onion-shaped bell tower and surrounded by the village graveyard overlooking the village. Fifty-nine peasant houses, half on each side of the road, all resembling each other with red tiled roofs and lined up closely, occupy the space between these two landmarks. And on a path branching off to the east

The partisan monument at the entrance to Žerovnica. It names all the villagers who died in World War II.

at the northern end of the village stand the five larger and more imposing millers' houses and their mills, all strung along the Žerovniščenica stream. To the south, in the surrounding mountainous terrain, stands another landmark on the highest peak: the ruin of the former feudal castle Šteberk from where the count, now a mythic figure in village lore, once ruled over the villagers, owned the land they cultivated as well as the forests and to whom they once owed corvée.

Circling the village are the until recently well-kept, symmetrically laid out, narrow strips of land that subdivide seven large fields. They were tilled following a system of crop rotation (*kolobarjenje*) inherited from the feudal period. Crops included wheat, rye, barley, oats, clover, potatoes, and various kinds of vegetables for animal and human consumption. The hay fields of the villagers, laid bare when the Cerknica lake drains in summer, abut the strips of land and reach all the way to those of the cooperative farm Marof, the Cerknica lake, and the highly valued forests.[2]

I did not then realize how deluding the ideal, normative view of the villagers was, expressed by common comments such as, "We are a friendly village, we are all alike, and everyone has the same amount of land." Today it would be hard to find a peasant who would agree that such statements

Sveti Pavel (St. Paul) church, overlooking the village

had ever been accurate. And even in the sixties, as I was soon to learn, such assertions concealed the realities of inequities of wealth and power and complex, often tension-ridden social relations in the village. They also masked ideological differences between the majority of anticommunist peasants and the minority of poor or landless peasants, some of whom identified with the communist bureaucracy, the impinging state-run institutions, and the Slovene state apparatus in general. The following passage from my original study describes how the village appeared to me and my family in 1964:

> The road from Grahovo leads to the northern entrance to Žerovnica, marked by a bridge over the Žerovnišča River, which here borders a small village green, the only common gathering place today. The green is shaded by the wide boughs of a linden (*lipa*) tree, beneath which there are a few benches and a table. Alongside the linden tree rises a partisan monument. Next to the monument is the *balina* field, where a few men and boys meet on evenings and Sundays to play the *balina* game, a form of lawn bowls. It is found everywhere in this area and is a recent introduction from Italy.

The central road leading from the green is faced by houses of plastered stone, many of which need paint. To each house is affixed a shiny red plaque bearing a number. Villagers, however, have never learned the numbers so convenient for the tax collector; their dwellings are still identified by traditional house names, registered in the earliest church records. Houses are fronted by wooden benches and some by small, fenced-in flower and vegetable gardens. Behind each house are attached sheds for fowl, pigs, cattle, and horses, next to which are storehouses. . . . The manure pile, used for fertilizer, is close by. Generally, there is another shed that houses a special stove on which to cook feed for pigs, and, with few exceptions, there is an outhouse. Then come the fruit trees—apple, plum, and pear—and finally the detached storage barn (*skedenj*) where hay and cattle bedding is stored. Behind the homesteads are paths leading to the fields, where wheat, maize, fodder crops, potatoes, beans, and other vegetables are grown.

On a spring afternoon a few elders sit on benches in front of their houses. Small children play along the road, in the stream, and under the linden tree on the green. A villager with his ox-drawn cart, carrying his wife and children and perhaps one or two grandparents with their hoes and rakes, leaves for the fields. All but the very old and very young are at work, and the village is quiet and empty. The road leads through the village to the hill on which the church stands and near which is the oldest structure in the village, a traditional storage barn (*skedenj*). Anyone climbing the hill is rewarded with another excellent view of the area. In the churchyard, enclosed by an old stone wall, are the family graves of the villagers as well as a collective grave of seven partisans. The bell in the baroque, red-painted steeple no longer rings, but the church itself is freshly whitewashed. Until the autumn of 1964 Sunday masses were celebrated in Žerovnica. Now they are celebrated only in Grahovo. (1971, 23–27)

Such an immediate impression of a bucolic and peaceful scene is misleading. A more realistic portrait of the village in the sixties would have noted that the castle on top of the highest peak, once inhabited by the local feudal lord, is a neglected ruin, a signal of the past. The church of St. Paul (Sveti Pavel) on the hill was no longer allowed its own parish priest but had to make do with the priest from Grahovo, the neighboring village, and who came to Žerovnica for a Sunday mass that the youth rarely attended.

The neighboring cooperative farm (*zadruga*) Marof did not receive a favorable review from me even in 1964. The villagers regarded the concentration of power such units had as a menace to their private land because it afford the sole outlet for essentially all the peasants' products, leaving them with little bargaining power. The unenthusiastic laborers on the cooperative farm from the southern republics of Yugoslavia were viewed with considerable contempt by the villagers who thought them lazy, inefficient, and less civilized than themselves. They despised the Communist Party members from the city who had little knowledge of farming and held the administrative posts on the cooperative farm. The precommunist traditional private markets were no longer held, and Marof and the Brest furniture factory controlled the prices, although the peasants still traveled many miles to sell piglets privately, albeit for meager returns. Brest controlled prices for logs and boards, and of the five village saw mills that lined the Žerovniša stream only one was allowed to function, and that only marginally. In the 1980s Marof went bankrupt in spite of its large holdings and modern equipment. Yet the hardworking peasants, laboring under discriminatory policies, with their primitive equipment, ox-drawn plows and wagons, and little mechanization continued to be productive. The swollen bureaucracy of political functionaries running Marof and the wage workers' lack of motivation was the villagers' disdainful explanation for the failure of this ambitious government project.

After the fall of communism and the dissolution of the Yugoslav federation, the furniture factory Brest in nearby Martinjak also went bankrupt, but another branch in the district center Cerknica survived. Both, within easy commuting distance by bicycle or moped from Žerovnica, had complemented emigration as a supplementary source for economic survival since the end of the nineteenth century. In the postcommunist years other means of making a living such as learning a skill or profession and taking part in the plans for tourism have gained prevalence.

Notwithstanding first impressions, the houses that had all appeared so much alike turned out not to be so similar at all. Indeed, the interiors of the larger millers' houses by the stream, where the waterwheels once powered the saw and flour mills, were furnished with rugs and heavy, carved furniture, evoking the former wealth of their owners. Furthermore, while traditional crop rotation inherited from feudal times was still largely followed, it did not mean that all villagers could participate. For not only was land unevenly divided, but some villagers remained essentially landless and occupied themselves with village specialties such as carpentry. On average, a family held a quarter *zemlja* (fifteen hectares) of land,[3] and their owners were called *četrt zemljak* (quarter lander).[4] But a small number of peasants, who claimed to descend from the original founders, still owned a half *zemlja* (thirty hectares). At the same time, some held less than a quarter *zemlja* or no land at all.

Inequalities of political power accounted for village factions as much as did inequalities of wealth. After the demise of communism, this structure, as will be described in chapter 5, changed dramatically.

Historical Factors, Slovenia: The Official Record in the Communist and Postcommunist Period

As World War II concluded, Tito's Federal Socialist Republic of Yugoslavia was formed. For a short time after the war, before its break with the Cominform, the communist regime tried to collectivize the peasants. But the peasant families strongly resisted this policy, and consequently only a few large cooperative and state farms were organized in Slovenia, generally located on confiscated large landed estates and employing landless workers from the southern republics (Bosnia-Herzegovina, Montenegro, Kosovo). State policy concerning private peasants shifted to various attempts to obliterate their autonomy and traditions, dissolving local units into larger administrative formations controlled by urban bureaucrats. However, even before Slovenia achieved independence in 1991, some positive changes for peasants were introduced. In 1972, they were finally granted the right to take part in the health insurance and pension plans of the Slovene Republic, although pensions for peasants did not equal those of wage earners.

Revolutionary changes for Slovenia came as Europe entered the new age ushered in by Gorbachev's *perestroika* and *glasnost* and by the collapse of European communism. The Yugoslav Federation turned to civil war involving all the republics of the federation. Yet Slovenia attained its independence from Yugoslavia with only a limited degree of violence when the Serbian forces briefly attempted to stop this movement during the ten-day war in the summer of 1991. This raises the question why Slovenia was so privileged as compared to Croats and Albanians in Serbia, Serbs in Croatia, and the Muslims of Bosnia-Herzegovina, all of whom have been suffering from the violent aggression of "ethnic cleansing."

Answers to the question why Slovenia escaped most of the struggle and yet won its independence involve factors of geographical location, language, and cultural traditions that mark Slovenia and the Slovenes as somewhat different. Slovenia itself is the westernmost and northernmost of the former Yugoslav republics, sharing borders with Austria, Hungary, and Italy. The Slovene language, though South Slavic, is distinctly different from Serbo-Croatian, which is essentially one language in spite of the ideological investments on the part of both Serbs and Croats in minor distinctions of a lexical and orthographic nature. In addition, the Slovene language is highly valued, having a strong role in self-identity in this small republic of only two million inhabitants. The Roman Catholic religion, which the Slovenes share with the Croats, is not practiced in the rest of the former Yugoslavia, where Eastern Orthodoxy is the traditional religion of the Serbs, Montenegrins, and Macedonians; and many inhabitants of the former southern republics, Serbo-Croatian–speaking Bosnians and Herzegovinians as well as Albanians, converted to Islam after the area fell to the Turks in the battle of Kosovo Polje (Ravens' Field) in 1389. Most importantly, Slovenia, unlike the other republics that formed the Yugoslav federation, is ethnically quite homogeneous, with only a limited number of non-Slovene groups, primarily Italians.[5] The inhabitants of the few small Serbian enclaves in Slovenia have not identified with the Serbian nationalistic drives. And practically no Slovenes live in the other republics of the former Yugoslavia. The fact that Slovenia has the richest natural and industrial resources of all the former Yugoslav constituent republics has proven a double-edged sword for the country. On one hand, it was of considerable value to the Yugoslav federation, but at the same time the Slovenes, who often characterize their republic as the Switzerland of the South Slav lands, expressed resentment at what they considered exploitation by their poorer neighbors.

The Story of the Village

During the communist years peasant families worked hard, farm equipment was undermechanized, and rising taxes burdened the villagers. Additionally, villagers lost control over the products of their labor that were entirely regulated by communist enterprises. And after independence they lost their major markets in other republics of the former Yugoslavia embroiled in the ethnic conflicts in which the most powerful combatants were Serbia and Croatia. Thus Slovenia has attempted to increase the quality and diversity of its products to compete with the West. As in the past, few peasant families can manage without the help of at least one member working elsewhere, most commonly in the local furniture factory, Brest. Since the small strips of land owned by most families remain dispersed, farm work is laborious and the topography, thin topsoil and a stony karstic base, limits the use of large tractors and combines. Aging parents depend on help from the younger generation in cultivating the land but the youth now often work and live elsewhere. Consequently, the postcommunist village faces some difficult alternatives for the future, such as relying on tourism where the *občina* subsidizes favored families and there is little support for the elders in the formerly three-generational household. Yet the aim of the government is to preserve the architectural uniformity of the village as a tourist attraction.

In 1992, when my husband and I paid our first visit to the village after the collapse of communism, the dirt road leading from Grahovo through the village had been asphalted. There were no more oxen to be seen dragging plows, but small tractors now did this job, and cars were everywhere. Indeed, almost every house had a car, a television, a refrigerator, modern plumbing, and a gas-burning kitchen range, where only very few had such equipment in the earlier years. While preserving a certain exterior uniformity, the difference between the new remodeled houses, rebuilt with aid from the local government in preparation for tourism, and the rundown traditional peasant houses, was very great indeed.

Slovene Settlements in the United States:
Cleveland, Its Environs, and Hibbing, Minnesota

A brief review of the official history of the Slovenes in Cleveland will set the stage for the strong contrast between the vibrant and active life of the Slovene Clevelanders who were poor peasants in their homeland and the hardships and collapse of social and cultural life in Žerovnica under communist rule. The official depiction of historical events is an exemplar of the limitations of official records that do not let us into the minds and hearts of the migrants, after obfuscating their struggle to adapt in a strange country. An outpouring of activities by the ethnic community did not simply appear in the New World; rather it suggests that the villagers brought with them from Slovenia traditions of courage, stubbornness, industriousness, and an appreciation for cooperative labor and cultural activities. These persisted in the mind-set of the villagers but were largely inhibited by the communist regime in Slovenia.

I recount here some of the high points of the history of the ethnic Slovenes as they bear upon the Clevelanders. Beginning in the 1890s, there were two early, divergent streams of immigrants, the traditional Catholic one and the socialist one of secular orientation. Poor peasants motivated by economic necessity comprised both groups, and gradually the two grew to accommodate each other. Anticommunist immigrants left Slovenia after World War II for political reasons, and the rift between them and the earlier peasant migrants manifests itself through separate institutions and recreational parks. There was also an emotional barrier between members of the two waves of immigration since the early peasant migrants often maintained nostalgic recollections of their homeland, while the political migrants hardly shared such an affect. This study concentrates on the early migrations.

How is an urban ethnic study initiated? Boundaries between villages are anything but firm, and demarcations between urban and rural, and nation and state, although never as rigid as once thought, have become increasingly permeable and shifting. Today's demands by ethnic groups for cultural and/or political autonomy are often met with severe resistance by the nation-states of which they are a part. The American ideal of acculturation and the melting pot is being replaced by multiculturalism, which is a general term covering the most divergent developments and conflicts. One is not sure what the term *multiculturalism* signifies. Is it a new kind of ethnic separation, or are there some remnants of the official traditional American view that acculturation will simply enrich the many groups within a nation-state?

My first preparatory step was to obtain from the villagers lists identifying relatives or friends they knew of in the Cleveland area or elsewhere in the United States. I then consulted relevant documentation collected in the University of Minnesota Immigration History Research Center archives.

(Top image) Slovene immigrants sending supplies to Yugoslavia during World War II. *(Above)* Ethnic Slovene women sending food home. Each box displays the name of a particular village.

Finally, I conferred with a group of scholars at Cleveland State University who were associated with the Cleveland Ethnic Heritage Studies Development Program, a program engaged in research concerning ethnic groups in Cleveland. This provided me with a guide to the wide activities in the Slovene community and to the publications of the numerous Slovene institutions created in Cleveland. I learned about the varied and rich activities of the Slovene Americans, ranging from cooperative insurance organizations to social support groups in the Slovene homes described in chapter 5. I never encountered similar activities in Žerovnica or other Slovene villages I visited, although there were such cooperative efforts under Austrian rule.

Many migrants started their lives in the United States by lumbering and mining work in Pennsylvania, living in boarding houses there and during the early years in Cleveland, saving money until they could establish their own living quarters. When I first visited the ethnic community of Cleveland in 1973, I was struck by the fact that here, in the midst of a blighted American industrial inner city, I saw a dynamic community that in many ways modeled itself after the typical Slovene village, even though houses were constructed of wood and not of stone. Homes were fronted by the ubiquitous wooden bench and flower gardens, and towering above the settlement was the principal Slovene Catholic church of Cleveland, St. Vitus (Sveti Vit), built by the Slovene community. Some of the earliest Slovene homes stood on St. Clair Avenue, one being the spacious residence of the Grdina family, which the family had run as a boarding house in the early settlement days and which became—due to the hospitality of the Grdinas—an open house with coffee and sweets for all new Slovene immigrants. When my husband and I first saw St. Clair Avenue in the early 1970s, it was lined with shops and restaurants touting Slovene specialty items and food with large Slovene signs. Interspersed we found buildings that housed the principal Slovene mutual insurance fund, SNPJ (Slovenska Narodna Podporna Jednota), the Cleveland Slovene newspaper *Slovenska domovina* (The Slovene Homeland), the Slovene meeting house and club, the Slovene National Home (Slovenski dom), and a Slovene funeral home established and run by the Grdina family, Slovene leaders since the earliest Slovene settlements. An atmosphere of openness and friendliness pervaded the settlement.

My methodology in the Slovene communities of Cleveland and Hibbing, Minnesota, where a small settlement emerged due to work in the copper

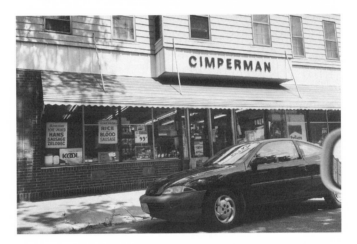

(Top image) The Slovene Workmen Association on St. Clair
Avenue. The sign is capped by a Pepsi advertisement—an
explicit montage. *(Above)* A Slovene food store on a side street
abutting St. Clair.

mines, did not differ radically from that employed in the earlier village study, although my aims, general orientation, and theoretical stance had by then shifted in the direction of a semiotic perspective. In Cleveland, both my husband and I were almost uniformly accepted as friends since I had written a book on a Slovene village, and since many came from the area of Žerovnica or had relatives there. We carried on open-ended, relaxed conversation, unguided by me except for my marked interest in life histories. Informants were all too happy to describe their past adventures and participation in events of all kinds. I taped almost all interviews, something I could not do in Žerovnica due to the general feeling of unease and guardedness that stemmed from the communist years but carried over into the 1990s. In Cleveland, only one of my older informants in the Slovene American community with close relatives in Žerovnica continued to express some unease, and consequently I did not use a tape recorder in these conversations.

Hospitality overflowed in Cleveland, just as it had in Žerovnica. Typically, Slovene Clevelanders and Hibbing Slovenes wished to relate their own or their family members' early experiences as migrants to the United States, recounting early hardships, life in crude dormitories, and long hours of work in the mines. The many ways in which the ethnic Slovenes helped each other during the early times of adversity surfaced as a repeated motif. Recurring themes among the older generation were nostalgia, pride in the homeland, and a strong desire to make Slovene history and traditions known.

On the basis of my observations and many conversations, I became aware of both parallels and transformations in old traditions. Values, attitudes, and institutions had changed the meanings of certain objects. Utilitarian in the home village, they were associated with highly emotive and aesthetic functions and significations in the new environment. Moreover, in the new and modern setting of the ethnic communities, one finds the preservation or revival of traditions long suppressed in communist Yugoslavia, as for example organized cooperative agencies and social activities.

After the early struggle there was considerable upward mobility among Slovene Americans in the 1970s. Some families would not leave the old Slovene settlement on St. Clair Avenue, but others moved from the inner city into typical American suburbs such as Euclid, Collingwood, and Newburgh, now largely inhabited by Slovenes who continue to participate in, or even lead, various ethnic societies and who support another Slovene Catholic Church, St. Lawrence (Sveti Lovrent). Some Slovene Americans were able to buy land and become farmers, again in many ways modeling themselves and their farms after the homesteads in the village, notwithstanding the much larger land holdings and the higher degree of mechanization. It also became clear that, from the point of view of the Slovene ethnic community, there was a hierarchy of "others" in Cleveland, namely the aforementioned later political anticommunist Slovene immigrants, as well as Croatians, Czechs, Italians, and African Americans. In-group feeling was strong. The younger generation's feelings of identity were more complex, showing the strains and positive effects of their transnational heritage. They wished to be Americanized, adopting trendy clothes, expressing typical American interests in sports and films, but they also expressed an awakening interest in their Slovene cultural heritage and wished to revisit the home villages of their parents or grandparents.

I now turn to the small Slovene community in Hibbing, Minnesota. In 1976 we visited Marija Lunka in Hibbing. She was the sister of the former *podžupan* (headman) of Žerovnica, Matija Rok, who had been our chief informant and friend in the sixties and seventies, and who is now deceased. The copper mines, which had drawn Mrs. Lunka's deceased husband to this northern Minnesota community, were by then exhausted, and the land scarred by strip-mining was barren and desolate. When my husband and I arrived for an announced visit with the *gospodinja*, Mrs. Lunka, we were met by all her family gathered in the living room of her comfortably furnished ranch-style house.[6] Family pictures hung on the living room walls, but the primary wall decoration was a hoe the *gospodinja* had brought from Žerovnica decades ago. Her daughter was married to a Slovene American who had achieved a position in the city administration. The *gospodinja* recalled how her husband had preceded her to America and then sent for her, the backbreaking nature of the work in the copper mines, and her husband's disappointment at his rude awakening to the realities of the American Dream.

At the time of our last visit to Cleveland in 1995, it was clear that some Slovenes were already entering the commercial and middle class, and, as I discuss in more detail in part 4, that the St. Clair neighborhood showed strong signs of disintegration under the impact of the inner-city blight. The strength of the St. Clair area was upheld primarily by the St. Vitus church, the largest Catholic church in Cleveland, the large Slovene National Home (Slovenski dom), with meeting rooms and places for celebrations of all kinds, and the Slovene National Library (Slovenska narodna čitalnica). Yet many members of the younger generation had moved to largely Slovene suburbs, and there was no move on the part of Cleveland city officials to perpetuate or restore the traditional Slovene community.

Conclusions

I wish in this study to render a semiotic analysis of the interrelations of two communities, the Slovene village and the Slovene ethnic communities in America in Cleveland and Hibbing. I believe that this is possible since I have now thoroughly studied both groups, the villagers of Žerovnica since the 1960s, and the Cleveland and Hibbing Žerovnicans since the early 1970s. Repeated field research in Slovenia and Cleveland has given me the advantage of a double perspective, enabling me to interpret evidence of cultural behavior transformations and revivals of past practices in Cleveland. Letters, visits, and, indirectly, memorabilia, have sustained constant contact between the two groups over a long period of time. But objects have taken on new meanings. On our last return to the village in 1995, Tone Primožič, the husband of Mrs. Lunka's niece, Marija, who is the daughter of the late Matija Rok, told us of the fate of the Žerovnica hoe that we had seen as a decoration on the living room wall: "Do you know that Mrs. Lunka insisted that when she died the hoe should be buried with her? And so it was! It is now with her in her grave."

It is important to note that the Slovene example shares characteristics with some other ethnic groups in the United States, including Polish groups in the United States and Brazil. Yet the closeness of the attachment between the Slovene village and Slovene American communities remains marked.

II

Theoretical Issues and

Terminology:

From the Outer to the

Inner Point of View

Chapter Two

Nationalism, Ethnic Identity,
Transnationalism: *Issues of Terminology*

Society and Nation

In his strong critique of the conventional understanding of such terms as "society" and "nation," Eric Wolf held that the term "society" connotes a Western bourgeois and Marxist view of the modern nation-state that, through its power advantage, indoctrinates its members with the ideology of common social and moral values. These then become the essence that cements the totality with society conceived as a bounded and homogeneous whole made up of interacting units (1988, 752–61). This does not satisfy Wolf, for such a view assumes that one society or nation necessarily shares one culture and one history. Rather, Wolf argues that, from primitives on, intersecting and fluid networks created by various changing bonds are the more ambiguous, more complex, but also more realistic phenomena that characterize societies. Decrying traditional architectural metaphors to describe "nexuses of interaction," Wolf invokes Lacan's "upholstery" (Lacan 1966, 502 as quoted in Wolf 1980, 757) that, through its spaced buttons, designates key points in chains of significations, a metaphor that exemplifies the kind of inventive leap that anthropologists might emulate.

For Wolf the concept of society has "become a hindrance in our search for more knowledge" since "it sets itself up as an eternal verity" (1980, 759). But, he warns, dissatisfaction with this concept as a total system should not lead to substituting for it the individual as a total system. I quote Wolf's comment in full because it leads to concepts I shall discuss later. Wolf sees neither society *nor* the individual as a timeless essence. For Wolf, the

> abstract individual is merely another monad, a timeless and reified essence like the conceptual entity it is supposed to criticize and oppose. Real-life individuals, in contrast, in the many different cultural settings that we know

about, are differentially constructed out of ancestors, parents, kinsmen, siblings, role models, spirit guardians, power animals, prenatal memories, dream selves, reincarnated spirits, or gods taking up residence in their heads and riding them like divine horsemen. . . . We need to invent new ways of thinking about heterogeneity and the transformative nature of human arrangements and to do so scientifically and humanistically at the same time. The attempt to understand what humans do and conceive economically, politically, socially, morally, cognitively and emotionally all at once has always been a hallmark of anthropology, and the goal remains a usable and productive program. (1980, 760)

Wolf's position, which sees the individual as a heterogeneous unit with many identities, is particularly relevant to transnationalism, a concept that resonates with the much earlier Peircean human sign grounded in the perception of the self as "other," and with Bogatyrev's and Lotman's notion of multiple identities, which I take up in chapter 4.

In another critique, Rabinow considers the terms "society" and "modernism" as questionable forms of nominalism (1988, 355–64). Since "society" acquired its current meaning as a quasi-natural or universal term in Europe in the early decades of the nineteenth century, we have a new object which is symbolized by new norms and new forms as well as by practices associated with it, all of which attempt to localize society and thereby regulate and represent that new reality "so as to produce a healthy, efficient, productive functional order" (360–61). In Rabinow's critique all elements of society are combined into a representable object, the modern planned city, "as a regulator of modern society . . . one of the most complete exemplifications of modernity" (361). These norms and forms of society are becoming increasingly autonomous, freed from previous constraints "claiming a historical and an acultural universalism" (362).

The concept of modernism, Rabinow holds, needs to be revised. Rabinow wishes to see a kind of modernity that is a possibility and that nevertheless has not dispersed into postmodernity. For Rabinow expects from anthropology a kind of practice where one must learn "some-thing," but asks, "how can the fragmentation of bourgeois culture, through the undermining of its claims to universality in which cultural anthropology has played an important role, be overcome, opened to world horizons, and thereby be re-universalized?" How are we to avoid the present postmodernist situation where we are left with nostalgic ethnographies "with nothing to teach," just "self-cultivation of the anthropologist" and a kind of tolerance? "Although we do learn from this anthropology how different things can be, it is silent about who we are," he writes (359). Since anthropology has ceased theorizing, it does not offer an understanding of the other or ourselves: "offering no diagnosis of what it sees in the world, it fails . . . to deliver on the [Kantian, Boasian, Benedictine] promise to teach us some-thing with cosmopolitical import" (360). Rabinow concludes his critique with Baude-laire's ironic injunction, "you have no right to despise the present" (as quoted in Rabinow 1988, 362) and by endorsing Foucault's call for writing a *history of the present* which requires a self-reflective critical awareness (362). Like many of us, Rabinow would clearly like to see some kind of new synthesis. He rejects postmodernism as being simply fragmentation and modernism as being based on an empty kind of universalism. Thus he presents us with a focal dilemma of our day: What do we mean by cultural relativism?

Ethnicity and Transnationalism

The relation of the concept of ethnicity to the modernist and postmodernist issue and to semiotic concepts is complex. Indeed, what do we mean by ethnicity? Clearly, ethnic identity has today become highly ambiguous. Here Tambiah's view of ethnicity as embracing a label not only of minority or marginal groups but also of majority groups within a nation is most relevant. Referring to modernism, Tambiah comments, "the time of be-coming the same is also the time of claiming to be different" (1988, 348). How can these two positions complement rather than destroy each other?

I pause here to reflect briefly on the various perspectives that appropriate in one way or another the term "ethnicity." Dismissing genetic and cultural deterministic explanations thoroughly argued by Boas long ago (1940), the shift has been to the subjective, contextual, and changeable historical crite-ria. Glazer and Moynihan (1975) see the new usage of ethnicity as "the steady expansion of the term "ethnic group" from minority and marginal subgroups at the edges of society—groups expected to assimilate, to disap-pear, to continue as survivals, exotic or troublesome—to major elements of a society" (5). As De Vos writes, "an ethnic group is a self-perceived group of people who hold in common a set of traditions not shared by the others with whom they are in contact" (1975, 9). And I wrote somewhat later "an ethnic group may employ any part of its culture to bring to the fore (what it perceives as) its own specific and unique characteristics, and such particularities are always seen in contrast (and opposition) to the characteristics of cultures of other groups" (1983, 119).

Indeed, the whole area of ethnicity is not clearly understood. Hofer has introduced the useful term "latent ethnicity" to express what he believes is the sense of Michael Fischer's comments quoted below:

> Ethnicity is a part of the self that is often quite puzzling to the individual, something of which he or she is not in control. . . . Insofar as it is a deeply rooted emotional component of identity, it is often transmitted less through cognitive language or learning (to which sociology has almost entirely restricted itself) than through processes analogous to dreaming and transferences of psychoanalytic encounters.

As Hofer has pointed out, rephrasing Bourdieu:

> The attempt to protect a text from being misunderstood . . . may have the effect that "the desire to twist the stick in the other direction, drives one into exaggerations," and the text "can be negatively influenced . . . and bear the marks of what one fights against." (1997, 92)

Hofer turns the argument around and asks if misunderstandings are necessarily harmful, suggesting that "maybe it is possible to regard diverging interpretations—which originate from various academic communities—as commentaries on the original one" (93). In response to the view that traditional elements will disappear in several generations, Fischer points out that

> there is, however, another more exciting possibility—that there are cultural resources in traditions that can be recovered and reworked into rich meanings for the present. . . . Much of the best ethnography has depended upon . . . empathetic searching, and . . . making this explicit can foster more powerful and realistic cultural critiques through juxtaposition. (174–75).

Fischer advocates "a reading of ethnographies as the juxtaposition of two or more cultural traditions" (175), a position which resonates strongly with the frame of reference of the semiotically oriented scholars discussed throughout this study.

Certainly, as the above authors make clear, we need other tools than those supplied by the positivist tradition so deeply embedded in American thought and the postmodern claims of incommensurability to understand how these complexities, including the world view, beliefs, and values of the actors studied, can be interpreted.

This brings us back to the challenge of today's volatile world. A fortunate formulation is the term "transnationalism." Transnationalism is exemplified, for example, by our Slovene villagers at home and abroad. The identification of villagers with an idealized and romanticized America, and the nostalgic position of immigrants remembering and preserving lost traditions while absorbing much of American culture, tells the story. Still, while transnationalism is a useful concept, it is hardly sufficient for our purpose. We need other notions and terms more penetrating as analytic tools to help us understand and decode the transformations, connotations, and tropes we encounter if we are to translate and interpret the polysemic and multifunctional practices that bear upon the multifaceted phenomenon of ethnic meaning. Thus Rosaldo's very useful overview of the term "transnationalism" is only a beginning:

> As an analytic tool, it leads us to discover and examine the social relations that cross borders and boundaries in the production of families, networks and institutions, policies, and nationalism and culture identities in a new location. It enables older concepts like nationalism, ethnicity, race, class, gender and differences to be reexamined in a new light by anthropologists of whatever persuasion. (1995, 9)

I refer now to recent attempts by scholars to recast the traditional terms questioned by Wolf and Rabinow and to grapple with the question of how we understand culture in the modern era and which difficulties this question presents.

The Invention of Tradition and Imagined Communities

Hobsbawm and Ranger's *The Invention of Tradition* (1993) primarily discusses society at large and essentially takes an outer point of view. In contrast to Boissevain, Hofer, and myself, whose findings demonstrate the strength rather than dissolution of various traditional customs, even when transplanted into a new environment, these authors dismiss the viability of indigenous traditions. Hobsbawm and Ranger's volume opens with Hobsbawm's introduction, from which I quote: "Invented tradition is taken to mean a set of practices, normally governed by overtly or tacitly accepted rules of a ritual or symbolic nature, which seek to inculcate certain values and norms of behavior by repetition, which automatically imply continuity with the past" (1). Hobsbawm extends the notion of invented tradition to the conscious revival and reinstitution of certain practices of use to the establishment by the state. He sees such revivals as "formalization and ritualization, characterized by reference to the past, if only by imposing repetitions" (4). His examples range from the Boy Scouts to the Nazis.

Hobsbawm and Ranger introduce several highly questionable dichotomies. They distinguish "the strength and adaptability of genuine traditions" from invented traditions since old traditions may be alive or revived (8), and they oppose "custom" and "tradition," the latter being invariant, even if invented, while custom has practical functions that do not preclude innovation and change (2). Hobsbawm supports his view by the example of peasant movements that claim some common land, a claim often without the weight of historical fact and simply an expression of a battle between village and overlords, or between villagers. In the case of the peasants from Žerovnica, however, the claim to specific lands is based on custom and genuine tradition, and therefore is not invented. To untangle the distinction between culture and tradition is clearly neither possible nor useful. Hobsbawm's second opposition, genuine versus invented tradition, leads him to state that "where the old ways are alive, tradition need be neither revived nor invented" (8). It is true that in their refusal to submit to oppression, peasantries have found ways to practice genuine, unapproved traditions unobtrusively. Such practices are far from invented.

Bakhtin's essential distinction between official ideology and indigenous life and its traditions and values is not made by Hobsbawm. Certainly those who felt themselves part of the Slovene nation suffered manipulation and oppression in communist Yugoslavia, and as we look at Slovene history, this was only the last of a long line of foreign rulers. But the Slovene example, which applies also to other formerly communist-dominated countries, shows that, from the point of view of the local population, communist ideology, in spite of attempts to indoctrinate and invent traditions, did not succeed. Slovene behavior, by and large, focused on preserving traditional behavior. Now, since the overthrow of communism, the revival of former traditions is beginning. For example, traditional carnival activity is now again an important performance event.

In considering the imposition of invented traditions by the power holders, we cannot exclude the more subtle, though often obvious, efforts by the capitalist and democratic West to inculcate new traditions through commercialism, advertising, and the media in general all at the disposal of an empowered elite that has taken advantage of the downfall of communist rule. And the global village phenomenon cannot be overlooked. As Hayden remarks in his study of nationalism in Yugoslavia, historians and anthropologists

> who are not devotees of particular nationalist causes have become quite good at uncovering the "invention of tradition" from an external perspective, sometimes to the mutual discomfort of the "peoples" who see the "authenticity" of their culture as challenged, as well as to the anthropologists doing the work. (1993, 63)

Benedict Anderson's study *Imagined Communities: Reflections on the Origin and Spread of Nationalism* (1991) shows some affinities to Hobsbawm's and Ranger's views. It considers the loss of power by empires and rulers in the last 200 years as they were overturned by populations whose indigenous ways (language, folk art, and other traditions) had been severely repressed. Anderson defines "nation" "as an imagined political community, imagined as both inherently limited and sovereign." Drawing on Gellner, Anderson states that "nationalism is not the awakening of nations to self-consciousness: it *invents* nations where they do not exist" (Gellner 1964, 169 in Anderson 1991, 6). However, reaching back into the past, local populations have found historical and mythical validation for their claims as nations. These claims do not simply come out of the air. The manipulations by colonial or dictatorial rulers of national or ethnic borders in Africa, the Middle East, Indonesia, the Balkans, or North America (in the case of Native Americans) have in most cases not succeeded in erasing indigenous rationals or their reformulation by local groups.

Anderson extends the notion of "imagined" so far that it becomes almost totalizing, overreaching Hobsbawm and Ranger's "invented" and thus diminishing its usefulness. The lack of face-to-face communities today does not necessarily mean that common remembered indigenous or related traditions are imagined or invented. Is such a contention not an oversimplification of the interaction between inner, long-remembered traditions on the one hand and oppression and manipulation from without on the other? One of the surprises that has arisen in the wake of ethnic studies is that the uniformity of the culture of the commercial West, imparted particularly through the media, has not wiped out the force of past memories among various groups. Indeed, the reverse is often true. Similarly, ideological indoctrination was easily shed in the communist-dominated countries, and the revival of past traditions was common. The turn of many formerly repressed groups toward chauvinistic xenophobia, however, introduces an entirely new dimension in which the revival of past histories and ethnic practices has turned into a banner for revolution and sometimes even ethnic cleansing (Hammel 1993a).

Boissevain and Revitalization

Boissevain advocates the strength of traditions when he quotes Manning: "Throughout both the industrialized and developing nations, new celebrations are being created and older ones revived on a scale that is surely unmatched in human history" (Boissevain 1992, 1). This is a phenomenon that has been little investigated. Boissevain calls for more case studies concerned with the revitalization of community celebrations and contrasts the case studies in his own collection with the findings of Hobsbawm and Ranger, pointing out that, since the articles in his collection deal with local and contemporary celebrations, they are not limited to invented rituals (2).

   Boissevain has found that some consequences of modernization have increased rather than diluted or destroyed traditions. While he admits that revitalization includes *invention,* he also points to the word's other connotations such as *revived,* or *reanimated, restored, resurrected,* and *retraditionalized.* Boissevain reveals that the 1970s emigration from southern to northern Europe tapered off, and that, in some areas such as Malta and Greece, considerable return migration occurred (8). The areas considered in his collection that manifest a return to traditional and ritualized performances are northeast England, Poland, Spain, Italy, Greece, and Malta. Some effects produced by modernization, industrialization, and unbridled economic growth and environmental pollution, as well as by the anomie entailed by these developments, have in various instances "led to a revalorization of 'traditional', often rural, lifestyles, including the rituals associated with them." As Boissevain notes, the media and growth of literacy have had complex results, not only those often deplored as destroying differences and replacing them with false values, but also the stimulation of rapid dissemination of ritual practices (8). Mass tourism has resulted not only in commercialization and the creation of "fakelore" but also in the participation of strangers, "an audience of others that has furthered the performative aspects of many celebrations" (9). In the case of Žerovnica, the construction of the electric pumping model of the "disappearing" Cerknica Lake discussed later and the performances that explain all its mysteries exemplify the amalgamation of tradition and modern technology that in fact serves to keep alive the traditions associated with the lake, albeit in a new form.

Boissevain emphasizes the increase of indigenous celebrations for the benefit of outsiders. The activities of regional residents presented before tourists, he holds, strengthen the local population's sense of ethnic identity. Boissevain writes that "as celebrations are invented, revised and retraditionalized, ludic activities are also increasing" (15). My own observations have confirmed the reemergence of traditions both in Žerovnica and in Cleveland and Hibbing. Boissevain predicts a circular trade-off: "As Europe becomes more unified in a single market, the homogenizing pressure of bureaucrats, media men, and commercial hucksters will also increase," generating in turn "more ritual activities as communities at various levels assert and defend their identities" (15–16).

That Boissevain's conclusions may have validity under various circumstances can be illustrated by my husband's and my experience in the fall of 1993. After attending a conference at the Masaryk University in Brno, the Moravian capital of the Czech Republic, we and other foreign delegates were taken on a bus tour of southern Moravia. First we visited the well-kept memorial to the battle of Austerlitz (a town now called Slavkov) in the field where the famous battle between Napoleon and the Russians took place in 1812. As we proceeded, our bus took us through a typical small Moravian village, with whitewashed houses lining each side of the street. We heard

oom-pa-pa music as a village brass band played, and we saw villagers dancing in the street in national costumes. The villagers jokingly prevented our
bus from proceeding, and we were insistently drawn into the dancing,
flowers placed into our button holes. *Hody* (a pig slaughtering feast) had
occasioned this particular celebration. While women were the most enthu-
siastic participants, the band consisted of men in national costumes and
other men, also in national costume, watched from their big horse carts.
The carts, the horses' manes, and the whips were decorated with ribbons in
the national colors. However artificial this performance may appear, it also
seemed quite genuine. As Herzfeld has remarked, "The nostalgia for a
balanced past perhaps explains the success of official kinds of folklore"
(1991, 45). Such traditions and ceremonies appear quite genuine, but they
probably have lost the spontaneity and full participation of former times.
Pig slaughtering ceremonies are widespread in Slavic Europe, an example of
which Minnich describes well in a study of a northern Slovene village
(1979). Thus the combination of modern commercial culture and the cultural revival of old traditions, even when they seem somewhat artificial,
cannot be ignored.

Fél and Hofer: East and West

The two-way relation between folk cultures and the urban elite is well
demonstrated in Fél and Hofer's remarkable study of Hungarian folk art
(1994), which illustrates the creativity of the local community in its struggle
against destruction or silencing by power holders. Fél and Hofer hold that
"East" and "West" present alternative concepts of national identity as well as
alternative concepts for the future. "West" means catching up with modernization with Western Europe, while "East" means preserving traditions and
protecting what is felt to be ancestral national identity (7), a notion well
supported by the rich fieldwork data from Fél and Hofer's ethnology of a
Hungarian village, Átanyi (1969), and by their more recent study. Hofer
writes that he does not mean to say that "Hungarians are absorbed in the
contemplation of history and that they judge the present by the past." But
although many know little of their history, "historical legends and heroes
are a part of daily life." He states that "the contrasting 'Eastern' and 'West-

ern' interpretations of Hungarian history can be used to express various views of the future. This is especially true of Hungarian peasant culture." Overlooking folk culture would be a mistake since, as Hofer writes,

> ancestral Eastern legends have become incorporated into national literature and art. . . . Hungarians wanted to differ especially from the Austrians of the 19th century. Apart from this, it is also obvious that different segments of society are in competition to be the "most authentic Hungarians." Each group formed and propagated different models of history and models of peasant culture in order to legitimate themselves. (1994, 8)

Thus interrelated and competing peasant symbols have affected the generation of national symbols, as have the conflicting meanings of West and East. For while the Slovenes feel Western, for example, they also consider themselves Slavic.

Conclusion: The Dynamics of Ethnic Identity

I hold with Fél and Hofer that the problem of tradition cannot be subsumed under one or a few concepts and must be seen both from an inner and an outer view as well as from the heritage of different national histories. An example of the dynamics of ethnic identity is the return to Slovenia of immigrant visitors, and particularly of Slovene-American choral societies that travel to Slovenia with the specific aim of reintroducing lost musical folk traditions. The Cleveland choral society *Zarja* has been touring Slovenia for decades, thus reintroducing part of a remembered heritage. It is then the villagers that compose the audience for the performance by visiting Slovene-American emigrés. From the point of view of the former communist bureaucrats such performances must seem ironic, since the centralized state and Marxist ideology had robbed the village of its traditions only to now witness their roundabout return, transforming village apathy into a celebratory remembrance.

We are led back once more to the broad issue of values in the postmodern world and the exploitation of ethnicity for power and domination. Hammel, whose pessimistic views I have alluded to earlier, deplores the loss of Enlightenment values. I reiterate my remarks from the introduction by saying that, unless analytical tools and theories help to give rebirth to a brand of humanism that combines rationalism, human rights, and diversity with peaceful self-determination, some pessimism may be justified. One needs to address Rabinow's warning that anthropology may have "nothing" to teach.

We are faced here with the old dichotomies (synchrony/diachrony, relativism/universalism) in a new form: Since in postmodern relativization we have the loss of all stable values, universalism is sterile scientism, and history is rewritten. Unless these trends can be reworked into a broader framework that attempts to understand the preservation of past values as not entirely lost to the global phenomena, a fruitful study of culture that encompasses its many dynamic and often ambiguous meanings is in danger.

I now turn to a discussion of some contemporary anthropologists who try to take an inner view and ask whether they are able to resolve some of the above dichotomies.

Chapter Three

Can We Find the Inner Point of View?

Interpretative Anthropology, Performance Anthropology

In the preceding chapter, I noted the inadequacy of traditional terminology and looked at some attempts to invent explanatory terms that do not distort cultural realities. I have appropriated the term "transnational," which comes to grips with contemporary cultural flux and where groups identify with more than one culture regardless of traditional boundaries or political barriers. Yet this term is so general that it becomes necessary to consider varied forms, ideologies, analytical tools, and concepts appropriate to, and most productive in, the task of interpreting different kinds of transnationalism that are embedded in the widely differing cultural traditions, experiences, and histories.

A primary question in this quest is how to determine the communicative object, the significant unit for the analysis of culture and cultures, from which one can try to construct the inner point of view. Here I employ Lotman's "culture text" as the significant communicative unit, modified in this study, where pertinent, to "transnational ethnic culture text." My term means texts that communicate ethnic identity in opposition to another ethnic group or distinct cultural unit. Transnational ethnic culture texts are binary by definition, but while most culture texts can be read as ethnic texts, all culture texts cannot necessarily be looked upon as ethnic texts, for much depends on the context. If a culture text such as a dictionary, which is essentially referential, is displayed proudly as a cultural document by an ethnic group, it may be interpreted as an ethnic culture text that celebrates a particular language as opposed to others. Furthermore, aesthetic and emotive functions then overshadow its referential one. In what sense then do interpretative anthropology and performance anthropology illuminate ethnic identity and the inner point of view?

Interpretative Anthropology

Geertz's interpretative anthropology, as his well-known article "The Native Point of View" (1983b) demonstrates, has as its goal the investigation of the inner point of view, an important effort, but not enriched by the semiotic notions of the scholars investigated here. Geertz utilizes the term "text" somewhat ambivalently and inconsistently. He notes that since the Middle Ages various views of "text" have freed the term from the confines of scripture and writing, allowing us to see all culture as an "assemblage of texts." Geertz also asserts that the idea of "text" "remains theoretically underdeveloped," and thus "the more profound corollary, as far as anthropology is concerned, that cultural forms can be treated as texts, as imaginative works built out of social materials, has yet to be systematically exploited" (1973a, 448–49). Here Geertz ignores the Moscow-Tartu group's concept of *culture text,* advanced since the late 1960s particularly in the works of Lotman, which are not additive as Geertz's "assemblage" implies. Nevertheless Geertz writes that "the concept . . . of culture I espouse . . . is essentially a semioptic one" (1973c, 5), but Geertz's semiotic does not reach, and even rejects, the ambitious theoretical dimensions implied by the Moscow-Tartu School.

Among the many appraisals of Geertz's interpretative anthropology are those of Crapanzano who is particularly critical of what he sees as Geertz's blurring of the boundaries between the authorial subject's voice and that of the interlocutors (1992, 63).

The problem of authorial voice and how it should be accounted for is a major issue in ethnology. Some of my ethnographic findings in Žerovnica illustrate the difficulties of obtaining what Geertz calls the "native point of view" and the authorial presence's elusive effect. Until the demise of communism in Slovenia, no villager would say anything derogatory about another although there were strong internal fissures between families, particularly between those of former partisans and those of the former *domobranci,* the Slovene group that fought the partisans and collaborated with the occupiers. Nor did villagers mention tensions between the larger and smaller land holders and the once well-off millers, between the usually landless communists in the village and the anticommunists who were in the majority, or between neighbors whose houses huddled together very closely.

Yet internal conflicts could be deduced from indirect and nonverbal signals such as intonation, facial expression, and general body language. Indeed, in our long hours of conversation, neighbors rarely mentioned each other despite the fact that a mere narrow path separated their homes.

Performance Anthropology: Memories of History

Turner's anthropology of performance also delves into the inner lives of the subjects he studied. While Geertz takes us through one key performance, the cockfight, Turner's performances, which he calls social dramas and which we can class as culture texts, are many. He sees them as rooted in Greek drama (1982, 11–12). Turner extends Van Gennep's concept of the liminal, which applies to tribal cultures, to his own term "liminoid" that refers to the carnival atmosphere in complex societies. Turner uses a hermeneutic spiral as his metaphor for cultural performances (14). While he does not write specifically about Bakhtin, similarities between their ideas are striking, particularly when it comes to Bakhtin's stress on pragmatics, performance, reflexivity, carnival reversals, and the grotesque in medieval society.

I limit myself here to only a few examples from Turner's writings. His studies of liminality in Ndembu male rites of initiation isolate one sector of society, the male one, from an opposing one, that of the female. This is or can be considered an ethnic division. The centrality of the grotesque, conveyed by juxtaposing noncombinables in masks and sculptures and by the miming of animals and supernatural beings, communicates sacred meanings. Turner insightfully observes that such distortions encourage reflections on categories and realities and thus enhance creative thinking (1964), a thought similar to Peirce's notion of binary index and the uncontrollable rush to conceptual thinking. Turner had many ideas of import concerning the marginal aspects of cultural behavior, but he accepted some underlying organizing principles in culture, such as basic symbols and beliefs, and his very own constructs of the "liminal" and the "liminoid" invite comparisons of differences and similarities in cultural behavior. He writes that

> whether as speech behavior, the presentation of self in everyday life, a stage or social drama, would now move to the center of observation and hermeneutical attention. Post-modern theory would see in the very flaws, hesitation, personal factors, incomplete, elliptical context-dependent situational com-

ponents of performance, clues to the very nature of the human process, and would also perceive genuine novelty, creativeness, as able to emerge from the freedom of the performance situation, from what Durkheim . . . called social "effervescence." . . . What was once considered "contaminated," "promiscuous," "impure," is becoming the focus of post-modern analytical attention. (1986, 77)

Turner writes that he hopes postmodern searches lead to the nature of the human process. He explores subtle channels, forms, and functions of the communicative act and the great ambiguities of interpretation that increase the richness of meaning, which he always sees in the framework of context. Experience for him is never completed until it is expressed and communicated to others in intelligible terms (1982, 13). This echoes Peirce and Lotman who wrote that communication implies a minimum of two interacting communicative units, but that messages do not exclude auto-communication.

Memory and History, and Comparisons of Comparables (after Boas)

The search for the inner point of view expressed in history and memory has become a focal issue in modern ethnology. We are impelled to acknowledge that official versions of history are only part of the story, and that the domains of history and memory seen from the inner point of view have their own reality and coherence.

Memory and history are interestingly considered by Connerton (1991), Bahloul (1993a and b, 1994), and Herzfeld (1991), and in these authors we can discover connections to semiotic concepts. Connerton's *How Societies Remember* (1988) postulates that meaning, not limited to the verbal realm, abides everywhere in culture. He strongly emphasizes nonverbal and particularly bodily sources of memory from the inner point of view, sources he believes have not received adequate attention. Connerton, following Halbwachs (1925, 1950), investigates the existence and sustenance of collective memory (1991, 1). For him, "our experiences of the present largely depend on our knowledge of the past, and our images of the past commonly legitimate a present social order" (2, 3). He believes ritual performances convey and sustain such memories. Connerton points to a wide area of bodily sources of memories and holds that this kind of behavior accounts in important ways for "inertia in social structures" (5). Yet he does not note the power of history and memory to energize groups that feel dominated by, and are rebelling against, a repressive past or present. Although Connerton is attracted to Bakhtin's carnival reversal of hierarchies, he considers them mainly as representing a utopia and does not take up the ironic and satirical critique of society in performances described by Bakhtin.

Connerton lists three types of memory claims, personal, cognitive, and habit, holding that it is the last type, habit, which has largely been ignored (25). He takes his examples of the repetition and persistence or transfer of social memory, particularly through commemorative ceremonies and bodily practices (40), from practices of the Nazis and those of major religions. But I counter that these examples are saturated with official ideology and do not necessarily reveal the inner views of ethnic subjects. Only in an official and artificial way can we consider them habits. Nor does Connerton take into account the highly polysemic aspects of memory expressed in sensory impressions. Thus Connerton's view that memories legitimate the present order is only part of the story. We should take note of Lotman's and Uspensky's lucid observation pertaining to the conflict between early Russian Orthodoxy and pre-Christian practices in Russian culture: here, pre-Christian forms of behavior persisted, functioning as legitimized antibehavior (1984, 9). As we shall see among the villagers at home and the ethnic immigrants, memory is a power force for the preservation of nonofficial history.

Of particular interest here is Bahloul's study *The Architecture of Memory: A Jewish Muslim Household in Colonial Algeria, 1937–1962* (1996). She examines the part played by memory and history in the intercommunication between two communities separated in space but related through kinship ties. They are French and Algerian Jews who once resided or still remain in Dar-Refayil, a multifamily house in Setij in eastern Algeria, where Bahloul's grandparents lived. Some migrated to Marseilles and Paris. She tells us that this house became the basis of a family epic and that she wishes "to explore the semantics of memory as it was articulated by an uprooted and dispersed group" (2).

Bahloul's work has some parallels to my study because prolonged dialogues between related but geographically distant communities that dramatically demonstrates the power of memory play a central part in both projects. Important differences between Bahloul's study and mine exist, however. Bahloul's is a doubly reflexive drama in which she mines the memories of her own ethnic group and relatives. Thus she observes not only the memories of two distinct grades but her own as well. I, of course, did not study my own migrating relatives. Furthermore, the historical and so-ciocultural differences between Bahloul's communities and those at issue in this study are considerable, for the Slovenes in Slovenia, while repeatedly conquered, did not have to cope with anything like anti-Semitism or the Holocaust, although they did suffer severe hardships during World War II. And the fate of the Slovenes in America, where the myth of the melting pot, illusory as it is, still implies the moral if not unchallenged obligation to tolerate diversity, differs sharply from the francophile idea of accepting those who reject diversity for the honor of being French.

Yet Bahloul's reception as an anthropologist also equaled mine. As she notes, her informants volunteered their stories willingly since they perceived her writing an academic book "as a chance to challenge official colonial history" (6). From her point of view her informants "became the heroes of what began to be perceived as a legend; their vanished world was about to be immortalized. I was transforming their banal story of ordinary people into an exemplary and heroic tale through the magic of the written word."

My recording of the stories of the Slovene villagers also depicted them in heroic roles, both from my and their point of view. The former local village head (*podžupan*), Matija Rok, whom I describe in detail in chapter 7, preserved historical village records in his house. Others found ways to beat the economic game by illegally selling baby pigs in private and by smuggling horses across the Italian border. Like Bahloul's informants, the villagers of Žerovnica also saw my book in progress as their version of history.

Calling upon Bakhtin and Yates (1966), Bahloul holds that "memory is conceived as a narrative art, *textual* in its structure" (133). She concentrates on memories of Dar-Refayil, identified by the name of the former Jewish owner who had died. The Dar-Refayil household was occupied by Sephardic Jews from 1930 to 1960, at which point they emigrated to France, but Muslims also lived there. Bahloul attempts to see memories and "mythological narratives, shaping the metaphor of the house as the material structure of genealogical history" (134). In Žerovnica genealogy is closely tied to size and structure, age and location of houses in the center of the village. These houses were, villagers say, constructed by first founders. In Žerovnica, the space and plan of houses, all so alike at first glance, had multiple meanings. From the kitchen to the master bedroom, from the shed with the animals to the *kuhinja* (cooking stove for the preparation of pig fodder), all reflected ancient traditions.

While Dar-Refayil was owned by Jews since the beginning of the twentieth century, the local French community imposed stringent rules as to its occupation, a fact that accounted for the gradual departure of most of the Jewish population who moved to the city of Algiers or to settlements in France. In striking contrast to the Slovene case, only a few subjects have returned for visits. Nevertheless, memory of Dar-Refayl is alive and is evoked when migrant Jews in the Jewish quarter of Paris celebrate life cycle rituals (141). The nostalgic recollection of the life at Dar-Refayil was not erased despite the difficulty of life there.

Herzfeld's *A Place in History: Social and Monumental Time in a Cretan Village* (1991) illustrates once more the inseparability of memory, place, and history, as well as the disruptive role, both positive and negative, of tourism. Herzfeld describes the reactions of residents in the Cretan agrotown of Rethemnos to state plans for a historical conversion to attract tourism. Not only do inhabitants distrust the plan; in Herzfeld's words, time is also contested, for "between social and monumental time lies a discursive chasm, separating popular from official understandings of history." Social time he describes as "the grist of everyday experience," while monumental time "reduces social experiences to collective predictability" (10). The state may declare Rethemnos a historic monument, but the town's residents do not necessarily want to inhabit a monument (10). Similarly, the transformation of Žerovnica into a tourist site and historical monument, does not reward the older peasants who do not benefit from the architectural changes to beautify a traditional village.

Clearly, economic strains are at work in both Crete and Slovenia, hence the turn to tourism. In Slovenia the problem primarily concerns the peasantry who is tied to its narrow strips of stony land and strains to eke out a living, but refuses to abandon the houses and fields their families have occupied for generations. Herzfeld's question, "who decides what constitutes the history of this place?" (227), equally applies to Žerovnica. The chasm between official and unofficial versions of history is dividing generations.

Chapter Four

Semiotics of Culture

In my investigation of the semiotics of transnationalism, I now turn to some converging concepts of the semiotically oriented scholars introduced earlier; they will serve as the guideposts of this chapter. 1) Peirce's four triads: Firstness, Secondness, and Thirdness; Sign, Object, and Interpretant; Icon, Index, and Symbol; Immediate, Dynamic, and Final Interpretant. Peirce's human sign, which is dependent on all the notions listed above, holds particular importance for my work; 2) Jakobson's metonymic metaphors and polyfunctional, polysemic messages; 3) Lotman's implicit and explicit montage, as well as the question of boundaries heroes; 4) Lotman's and Uspensky's memory and history, and their semiotics of everyday behavior; 5) Bakhtin's dialogic double-voiced discourse, and heteroglossia (which ensures the powerful role of context. I interweave with this discussion the creative thought of some American ethnologists who have applied and extended some concepts of Jakobson, Peirce, and Bakhtin.

These pivotal concepts, I argue, are fugue-like expanding variations that all resonate with Peirce's Third (the symbolic level of signs), even though Peirce was discovered by Jakobson only during his American years, was unknown to Bakhtin, and, until recently, unknown to Moscow-Tartu scholars. Roland Barthes lucidly describes the intertwining and intermeshing of concepts, arguing that intertextuality cannot be reduced to literary influence, for it composes the whole field of contemporary and historical languages as reflected in a text (Barthes 1975, 995). These themes unite the major part of this chapter. In the second part of this chapter I look at some postmodern interpretations and critiques of theories of culture, history, and the comparability of cultures. They often relate to but also contradict the semiotic approaches I discuss.

Saussure and a Brief Comparison with Peirce

The voluminous writings of American philosopher Charles Sanders Peirce (1839–1914) brilliantly outline the foundations for modern semiotics while the French-Swiss linguist Ferdinand de Saussure (1857–1915) first introduced the specific concept of a semiotics of culture. Neither Peirce nor Saussure could read each other's works since they appeared only after their respective deaths. Peirce's classic definition of the sign is "something that stands for somebody for something in some respect or capacity" (CP 2.228). Saussure defined the sign as a composite of a sound image (*signifier*) and a concept (*signified*), arbitrarily and inseparably related. Saussure's arbitrary sign or symbol should not be confounded with Peirce's Symbol. The latter is neither divided nor entirely arbitrary and linear; it is a general rule, rational, logical, and abstract, but modified by its hierarchical structure, that is its iconic and indexical levels. Peirce's sign is not dyadic as is Saussure's and cannot be understood except as a part of the triad Sign, Interpretant, Object. Saussure slighted the object and did not propose an interpretant. Insofar as he dealt in function, it was purely referential. Scholars today no longer generally accept Saussure's view that the sign is totally arbitrary but recognize that his stress on the arbitrary, from which he departed only in his *Anagrams,* was signally important to understanding cultures and languages, significant aspects of which are arbitrary. In his *Cours de linguistique générale* Saussure essentially considered language the model for all sign systems, yet even his famous outline for a possible semiotics of culture contained germs of a concept for nonlogocentric and even multifunctional roles for signs:

> By studying rites, customs, etc., as signs, I believe that we shall throw new light on the facts and point up the need for including them in a science of semiology and explaining them by its laws. (1966, 17)

Peirce

While Peirce did not specifically consider the context of culture in relation to signs, cultural practices were implied by what he called "habit." He was aware of different perceptions in different cultures, but his perspective remained essentially global. He investigated how humans perceive, think, and communicate within the broadest possible universal setting, and he thus referred to his opus as "pragmaticism," to be distinguished from a far more simplified and reductive "pragmatics." Fundamental to Peirce's *semeiotic* are his three categories, Firstness, Secondness, and Thirdness, for how the human perceives and cognizes the world is based on their interaction. Firstness is *monadic,* the mode of consciousness that is feeling, character- ized by immediate perception of qualities and the emotion that accom- panies this. It is associated with imagination, novelty, and originality and forms the basis for iconicity. Secondness is *dyadic,* the mode of conscious- ness that is volition, characterized by struggle, experience, and the emotion that these actions bring forth. Secondness, which yields the Index, is based on contiguity between individual objects, which includes *pars pro toto,* and thus, unlike Firstness, it is located in space-time. It must be binary, the most fundamental example of which is the idea of *ego* and the *other,* the basis of self-consciousness and of negation. Firstness and Secondness are two polar distinctions mediated by Thirdness, a power behind consciousness that accounts for an uncontrollable rush to perceptual judgment, essentially relationships, the level of the Symbol, and *continuity* (CP 5.90). One cannot overstate Peirce's Third and its salience for cultural analysis.

Peirce uses numerous variables to classify sign types. I shall limit my- self here primarily to the triad Icon, Index, and Symbol and to the human sign. An

> Icon by itself cannot act and consequently cannot be an Index, an Index by itself implies an Icon, but in itself has no meaning whatever: it is what it is by sheer chance. That is why a mental sign must be triadic: a Symbol, which necessarily includes an Index and an Icon. (Deledalle 1997, 3; see also CP 5.90 and CP 5.119)

It was Peirce who insightfully called for the investigation of the seeing oneself as object, a phenomenon he called "man-sign," a term which he invented (CP 5.532; cf. Portis-Winner 1983). He wrote that the "man-sign" acquires information and comes to mean more than it did before (CP 5.313). This did not escape Jakobson who noted that Bogatyrev, without knowing of Peirce's existence, realized Peirce's program, and "launched it over a century ago under the slogan 'Man, A Sign.'" It envisions the many roles every individual plays, and Jakobson urged that this program be furthered (1976, 30).

How, in practice, does the human become a sign? Peirce wrote that everything present to us is a phenomenal manifestation of ourselves, a fact that does not prevent it from being a phenomenon of something without us (CP 5.283): "When we think we are at that moment a sign . . . the man and the sign are identical" (CP 5.314). For Peirce "experience is our only teacher, its action takes place by a series of surprises, bringing about a double consciousness at once of an *ego* and a *non-ego* directly acting upon each other. An imaginary object was expected but something different comes instead" (CP 5.53).

The Prague Linguistic Circle in the Interwar Years and Jakobson's Postwar Years in the United States

The Prague Circle's "Theses" (1929) and Jakobson and Tynjanov's brief manifesto of 1928 rejected the Saussurean dichotomies *synchrony/diachrony* and *langue/parole,* as well as the notion of closed systems. The Prague School stressed the domain of internal speech. Prague School linguistics, under the influence of Bühler, distinguished speech functions according to their relation to certain factors. First come the communicative (referential) function based on the factor of context, second the expressive function focused on the sender and conveying the attitude of the speaker, and third the appellative function focused on the addressee (Bühler 1933, 147, 164). Additionally, the Prague scholars vehemently rejected the separation of linguistics from poetics.

Prague School semiotics also called for a systematic study of gestures, which had already been referred to by Saussure, and for the investigation of those relations among the interlocutors that effect the content and style of their communications such as their profession, their family, or the inter-relations between senders and receivers, etc. (Bühler 1933, 18).

It was not long before the concept of the sign found application not only in paralingual systems but also in clearly nonverbal systems. Bogatyrev's pioneering study of the semiotics of folk costumes (1976) was an early example. He concentrated on the changing functions and meanings of different costumes but also suggested a "general function" and a "structure of functions," which we would now call a metafunction, a function that comments on all the codes and functions of costumes that contribute to ethnic identity.

Mukařovský, a leading member of the Prague Circle, used the terms "semiotics" and "sign" in 1934 in his seminal *Art as a Semiotic Fact*. In his 1936 *Aesthetic Function: Norm and Value As Social Facts,* Mukařovský astutely distinguished between the norm-breaking role and the preservative role of the aesthetic function, a distinction that has held great value for ethnology as has his position that psychobiological universals underlie cultural worldviews and cultural expressions.

During his early American years, Jakobson broadened Bühler's three functions as well as the Prague group's poetic function by adding two more: the phatic function (a term borrowed from Malinowski), which focuses on the channel connecting the sender and receivers, and the metalinguistic function, which focuses on the code itself (1960b). Particularly remarkable was Jakobson's new formulation of his aesthetic principle:

> The poetic function projects the principle of equivalence from the axis of selection to the axis of combination. . . . Similarity superimposed on contiguity imparts to poetry its thoroughgoing symbolic, multiplex, polysemantic essence. . . . In poetry, where similarity is superimposed upon contiguity, any metonymy is slightly metaphoric and any metaphor has a slightly metonymic tint. Ambiguity is an intrinsic inalienable character of any self-focused message. . . . Not only the message itself but also the addressor and the addressee become ambiguous. (1960b, 358, 370–71)

Jakobson's metonymic metaphor, in its confrontation of unforeseen similarities, lends itself to a portrayal of transnational culture where two differing ethnic traditions are juxtaposed. His principle supplies the interpreter with a kind of double vision and is pregnant with possibilities for ethnological analyses.

Various American anthropologists have applied Peirce's and Jakobson's concepts to ethnological studies. In his notable *Man's Glassy Essence* (1984) Singer interprets Indian identity in Peircean terms. Singer writes that personal identity consists of feeling (Firstness), action (Secondness), and thought (Thirdness) (158). He notes that in Peirce's theory the self is not confined but may extend beyond the individual to social and collective identity (159), a position also held by the Moscow-Tartu group. Parmentier's primarily Peircean study *Signs in Society* (1994) attempts to put signs in ethnographic context by considering mortuary rites and mores in Belau. Caton not only authored a study of Jakobson (1987), he also applied the latter's semiotic concepts in his treatment of the Yemeni (1981).[1]

Jakobson's writings about Peirce are of focal importance since essentially alone he brought Peirce's work to the attention of American scholarship. Since Jakobson was half an anthropologist himself, he bore considerable influence on American ethnological studies. Jakobson's crusade began after his arrival in America. A short time later Jakobson asserted that Peirce's Legisign,[2] based on conventions established by human culture, was the essential difference between human and nonhuman forms of communication, writing

> that "a genuine Symbol is a Symbol that has a general meaning" and that this meaning in turn "can only be a Symbol" since "*omne Symbolum de Symbolo.*" A Symbol is not only incapable of indicating any particular thing and necessarily "denotes a kind of thing" but "it is itself a kind and not a single thing" for a Symbol only signifies though instances of its application through "*replicas.*" (1965a, 36; cf. Peirce CP 2.301)

Jakobson agreed with Peirce's view that the sign types Icon, Index, and Symbol are in fact interpenetrating levels of all signs, and that each type is distinguished by a different mode of being or grammatical tense: the Index by the past, the Icon by the present, and the Symbol by the future. Jakobson considered the Artifice, which he added as a fourth type to Peirce's triad, as atemporal (1965a, 36).[3] The interpenetration of the metaphor and the metonym is clearly a Jakobsonian concretization of the Peircean interdependencies of the three sign levels Icon, Index, and Symbol. The interpretation of objects and persons as metonymic metaphors proves useful to this study. For example, I interpret one of my important informers, an ethnic Slovene farmer, as a striking human sign. His bearing, every gesture, and language are metonymic or indexical of his village of origin and at the same time metaphoric or symbolic (or replicas or transformations) of the village mores.

The Moscow-Tartu School and Bakhtin

The authors of the Moscow-Tartu "Theses" on culture (1973) stressed the importance of the relation between the structural and the astructural.

> In the study of culture the initial premise is that all human activity concerned with the processing, exchange, and storage of information possesses a certain unity. (1.0.0) The mechanism of culture is a system which transforms the outer sphere into the inner one, disorganization into organizations . . . entropy into information. Culture moves from one sphere to another. It needs its outer sphere which it continually both destroys and creates. (1.2.0)

Lévi-Strauss also emphasized the important role of the astructural.

> We bear in mind the example of the natural sciences where progress from one structure to another . . . always lies in the discovery of better methods of structuring, by means of the small facts ignored in previous hypotheses as being "astructural." (1963, 327)

Culture Texts

The Moscow-Tartu concept of culture text owes much to the work of Pjatigorsky who defined text very broadly as a variety of signals composing a delimited, autonomous whole that must be spatially or otherwise fixed, and must be in some manner understandable (1962, 79). V. V. Ivanov, a leading member of the Moscow-Tartu School, called for the development of typologies for culture texts in all their varieties. One of the basic tasks for contemporary semiotics, he wrote, "remains the development of a general semiotic set of concepts and correspondences suited to the description of various sign systems, including those structured quite differently from the natural language" (1975, 218–19). While Western theoreticians, notably Ricoeur (1971a, b), Geertz (1973b), and Margolis (1993) have also applied and extended the verbal concept of text to culture in general, it was the Moscow-Tartu scholars who first submitted the concept of culture text to an extensive analysis, the "Theses" being only the beginning.

I shall not here present all the complexities of culture texts that the

"Theses" mentions and which have evolved over time (cf. Portis-Winner and Winner 1976 for a detailed discussion). Key concepts extremely useful for ethnological interpretations are those that Lotman "conjugates" through a grid: plot/nonplot, narration/nonnarration, and implicit/explicit montage. Lotman develops and exemplifies these concepts, the most central of which are artistic texts, in *Semiotics of the Cinema* (1976a). Lotman sees the filmic model as applicable to techniques of narration, themselves exemplary for all texts. As Lotman shows, the opposition implicit/explicit montage enables iconic pictures to act like discrete words, stimulating abstract ideas (1976a, 44–45). Similar techniques in ethnic nonverbal texts also permit simple objects to act like works of art. In implicit montage the compared elements are drawn from a common semantic domain but differ in modalities or grammatical meanings, which for Lotman include categories such as location, lighting, mood, size, and types of material. Internal transformation, and not addition of new elements initiate change in this type of montage. Lotman compared these montages to the kaleidoscope. Such texts are plotless, and narration is nonlinear. The changing expressions on a face in film exemplify one semantic domain that is conjugated into changing modalities. In explicit montage, on the other hand, the elements juxtaposed represent different semantic domains but share a common modality or grammatical meaning. Here, the addition of new elements that violate levels, and not transformation, is the key process (1978a). Eisenstein's film *The Strike (Zabastovka)*, where police agents have animal heads, and Turner's grotesque images and objects combining human and animal attributes in the Ndembo initiation rites may serve as examples of explicit montage. Texts exhibiting explicit montage are narrative, artistic, linear-plot texts, whereby Lotman bases the existence of plot upon a culture hero's crossing of boundaries. On the other hand, Lotman considers a plotless episode that may be part of implicit montage, essentially static, an event. In the spirit of the above montage types, Lotman contrasts culture heroes who cross borders to the more passive type that Lotman simply calls a part of the culture. An example of Lotman's culture hero in ethnic culture is the migrant who takes the initiative to cross borders and establishes for him- or herself a new transnational culture, or the peasant who circumvents the strictures of the communist regime and subversively devises means to sell on a furtive private market.

For the onlooker attuned to such tropes, dramatizations of montage in village and ethnic cultures are frequent. As I walked through the village and noticed threshing floors now no longer in use, villagers recalled that in "the good old times" a particular sound at threshing time, which they rendered as "*pica-poca*," was produced when three or four individuals threshed grain with a flailing stick at harvest time. The power of the sound stimulated nostalgic recollections, a remembered sense of well-being and cooperative activity at threshing time, a time always followed by a carnival-like dance, feasting, and villagewide celebration. Here I note that in Lotman's sense the simple repetition of a sound becomes a modality, bringing about the formal agreement of all other dissimilar elements from different semantic domains (Lotman 1976a, 58). Thus the material and practical meaning of the threshing sounds is muted and abstract and associative meanings are emphasized (45). The threshing sound adds a new dimension of meaning to elements not previously compared and one might say that the creation of a new set ensues.

Another example which may be interpreted as part of an explicit or implicit montage is the *kozolec*, a large wooden hay rack that dots the fields in Slovenia. In the new ethnic culture the *kozolec* takes on various forms, such as a toy, a small carved trinket, or a landmark in the Cleveland farmlands. Here the compared elements, the different manifestations of the *kozolec*, form implicit montages, taking their origin from one semantic domain but inducing abstract, associative meanings as a set. Recollections of village activities, threshing, hay rides, and landmarks, are all brought together by the modality of the changing shapes of the *kozolec*. On the other hand, when the *kozolec* is covered with hay and juxtaposed to a truck on which it rides in a Fourth of July parade down a Main Street in Cleveland, carrying a sign inscribed in large letters with the words "Heartland of Slovenia," the *kozolec* suggests an explicit montage, namely the juxtaposition of elements from very different domains. Again, this suggests new hidden similarities. At another level this performance may have a metaethnic function, commenting on what makes an ethnic Slovene in the United States. At the entrance to one of the farmlands created by the last wave of immigrants from the late 1940s stands an oversized *kozolec* made entirely from concrete, assuming the role of a monument. We can interpret this example as participating in an implicit montage if we place it with all the many forms of the *kozolec* found in Cleveland. But if juxtaposed to the many American markers mingling in the recreational areas, cars, American-style clothes, it can turn into an explicit montage. In the Žerovnica haylands the practical function of this structure predominates, but its aesthetic function also emerges for those with an artistic eye. *The Slovene Hayrack (Slovenski kozolec)* (Čop and Cevc 1993), an extraordinary book of photographs and text, illustrates this beautifully. Here the excellent photographs highlight the emotive and aesthetic qualities of this functional object.

Boundaries

Boundaries, in Lotman's sense, are never permanently fixed. Changing points of view of the culture bearers, the mythological perception of time and space, and basic values and semantic domains of the culture, all of which result in varying cultural evaluations and semantic interpretations of spatial units, can influence boundaries. Nonspatial as well as spatial relations can act as boundaries. Thus economic, religious, linguistic, or social distinctions, as well as kin or ethnic dimensions are frequently metaphorically spatialized (Lotman 1975a).

For its inhabitants, Žerovnica occupies the center of good internal space that includes upper, good space (the hill on which the church and the graveyard overlook the village) and, higher still, the decaying castle of the former count. Disvalued external spaces include the lower space, the dangerous sink holes in the karstic Cerknica lake, which have an important mythic role. Owing to the scientific study of the lake and the building of a model that explains its structure, the lake today has become a tourist attraction, and the traditional explanatory myths have lost their power.

For the villagers, the near and valued zone of internal space includes Cleveland and its rural surroundings but not a nearby Slovenian town that only sends tax collectors to the village. For Lotman (1995a), those living beyond the boundary, such as gods, the dead, other peoples, or strange animals, can occupy either of two zones in external space. Gods may be divided into "good" and "bad," associated with spatial orientations such as top/bottom or right/left. The upper part of external space may be the sky (heaven), which is good, its lower part can be the underworld, which is bad, while in the center lies internal space, the earth. In the ethnic Slovene community in Cleveland, the area that is physically lower, flats occupied by heavy industry and other ethnic groups, is undesirable, while that part of external space which is in fact in the higher hills, where the most desirable suburbs for ethnic Slovenes are located, is evaluated positively and transferred into internal space. Slovene settlers in the United States perceive their villages of origin, although distant, as internal rather than external space. In the same sense, an ethnic Slovene neighborhood in a Minnesota mining town, or a Pennsylvania lumber camp occupied by Slovene kin are potentially a part of internal space for Slovene villagers as well as for ethnic Slovenes in Cleveland.

Semiotics of Everyday Behavior

Most recently, the Moscow-Tartu School has directed its interests toward the semiotics of everyday behavior, humor, parody, and to new approaches to history. Lotman takes one of his examples from the eighteenth-century culture of the Russian nobility. During the reign of Peter the Great (1672–1725) everyday behavior, usually subconscious and considered natural by the actors, was often replaced by new patterns modeled on Western European aristocratic culture (Lotman and Uspensky 1984, 232). As a result, various Russian "styles" of everyday behavior from which the nobility could choose coexisted. Eventually the new patterns became theatrical in the sense that "an eighteenth century man would choose a certain type of behavior for himself" (241), a "role," a kind of "mask" (245). I see this description of role playing, the adoption of European styles by Russians, as a form of boundary crossing, implying an internalized transnationalism, involving, as it does, two contrasting cultural traditions, one that the individual attempts to suppress and another which becomes the "semantic dominant" that the individual tries to enact (245). From an outer point of view this performance may appear as parodying the French model and metaparodying double coding.

Lotman and Uspensky counterpose everyday behavior in medieval Russia to Bakhtin's portrayal of laughter in Western European culture which he claims freed individuals from religious and social constraints and transported them into a world of popular carnival utopia that reversed and parodied the dominant socioethical hierarchy (Lotman and Uspensky 1984, 36–52).

Semiotics of History and Memory

The issue of official and nonofficial, subjective and objective history is central to Lotman and Uspensky's later writings (1984, 1985). For Lotman the Symbol that plays an important role in the memory of culture because it can transfer semiotic formations from one layer of culture to another, thereby attaining a unity-providing function (1987, 12). In this sense, the Symbol contains an archaic layer, an important factor in cultural memory. Here Lotman's Symbol can be compared to Peirce's Symbol where abstract reasoning is dominant but always modified by iconic and indexical levels.

We may interpret many objects as symbols in Žerovnica as well as in the ethnic communities of Cleveland and Hibbing: the symbolic message of the partisan monument at the entrance to the village; the oldest structure for hay storage in Žerovnica; the lump of coal that resides permanently in a special place on the desk of a former miner who is now a tradesman in Cleveland; and of course the *kozolec* both at home and in its imported forms in Cleveland.

Parmentier has given very interesting examples of symbolic structures in his study on Belau (1987). He distinguishes "signs in history" and "signs of history," using various examples such as the Ashanti Golden Stool that takes the form of carved narrative pictures or anthropomorphic monoliths in Belau. He cites the Prague School's position that "synchronically manifested signs can represent the sedimentation of diachronic processes." As Parmentier notes, signs can have both functions. In Žerovnica, for example, the oldest structure has an active role in the corpus of historical memories and tales of its history, but of course it also stands as a sign of history in Parmentier's sense (13–15). And the oft-mentioned *kozolec* is not only a sign and marker of historical practices, but in Cleveland it becomes a "sign in history" for it is "extensively deployed in social action" (Parmentier 12).

The discussion of Parmentier's concepts pertaining to history intertextually leads us back to B. A. Uspensky, who questions the nineteenth-century view of history as a homogeneous and linear, monolithic progression of events (n.d.). As Uspensky holds, historical perception, since it is conceptualized from the point of view of the present, is based on a temporal mode that reverses the evolution of real events, that unfold from past to present, by proceeding from the present to the past. In spite of the fact that historical consciousness introduces time and cause into the stream of events, historical perception for Uspensky is analogous to perception in dreams. In a dream, a loud noise may provoke a sequence in which time flows backward in the dream, while the same event, if it awakens the dreamer, provokes a sequence in which time flows forward. The loud noise is the semantic dominant in the dream, "illuminat[ing] the preceding events which remain in our memory, determining how they will be read, . . . that is combining their causal connections instantly arranging them into a series with a plot" (8). The interpretation flowing from the semantic dominant establishes a point of view that acts as a "filter" through which images pass. Those not relevant disappear from memory, forcing us "to perceive all remaining images as connected and to arrange them into a plotted sequence" (8). Therefore, Uspensky concludes, "historical experience must be viewed . . . not as real knowledge which gradually accumulates in time . . . but as causative connections seen from a synchronic point of view" (9). Furthermore, since historical conceptualization of the past influences future events, the historical process is a sequence of steps from present to past and from past to future. Examples permeate the modern world. Sacred places in the Balkans and the Middle East act as semantic dominants, distorting events and rationalizing particular versions of history. Even the famous Statue of Liberty has come under discussion. Interpretations referring to the experiences of migrants from non-European cultures exist, thereby converting the statue into a sign in history as well as of history.

Both Uspensky's and Parmentier's observations affirm and tie into Lotman's acute insight about the relation of fundamental paradigms, namely chance and determinacy, that, rather than being incompatible, are two possible states. As opposed to physical science, "history is a process which takes place with interference from a thinking being." In historical processes not just chance but conscious choice thus becomes the most important objective factor (Lotman 1990, 232). Accordingly, historical semiotics must analyze how humans who make choices look at the world. The task is to reconstruct different ethnocultural types of such consciousness (231–32). Lotman's and Uspensky's analyses take into account that we live in a world where history from the official point of view is made and remade depending on the ideologies of power holders, and where the subjective history of local peoples may conflict with the ideological positions of power holders.

Lotman's Semiosphere

Lotman's concept of the semiosphere subsumes all aspects of the semiotics of culture, all the heterogeneous semiotic systems or "languages" that are constantly changing and that in an abstract sense, have some unifying qualities (1990, 125). For Lotman the semiosphere is not isolated from the rest of nature and is compared by analogy to V. I. Vernadsky's "biosphere," "namely the totality and the organic whole of living matter, and also the condition for the continuation of life" (Lotman 1990, 125 commenting on Vernadsky 1960, 102).

The semiosphere is asymmetrical, marked by strong differences between the center and the periphery (127), and involves a further development of Lotman's notion of boundary, defined as "the outer limits of a first-person form" where "our" space is safe and harmonious and "their" space is hostile and chaotic (131). The basic divisions arise from human biophysical and cultural criteria: the distinction of the living from the dead, the settled from the nomadic, or towns from countryside; the asymmetry of the brain; the rotation of the earth; the movement of stars; the cycle of seasons; constants of the human body; weight in relation to gravity; the opposition of up and down, right and left, male and female, or hot and cold.

Within this framework Lotman develops a semiotic notion of personality, recalling Peirce's human sign. While context is implied by Peirce, for Lotman personality is not separable from the cultural milieu. Thus a personality is not identified with a physical person alone but may include a group, property, and social, religious, or moral positions. For example, a master's personality may encompass his wife, children, and slaves. Clearly, as Lotman remarks, when differing views of the boundaries collide, disturbances occur (139). I have made examples of Lotman's network of personalities, which I call extended human signs, the subject of my final chapter.

Bakhtin's Dialogic Program

The recent revolution in American anthropology has cast doubt on the ethnologist's ability to represent. Inaccurately, Bakhtin is often seen as the source of the uncertainty and introspection haunting contemporary practitioners of anthropology. Bakhtin indeed sees representation as subject to interpretation, point of view, context, double voicing, and various ambiguous meanings, but he nevertheless holds that underlying chronotopic values and perceptions organize particular cultures. Universal factors therefore still influence particular cultural manifestations.

Bakhtin saw the significant units in human cultural communication as dialogic utterances in full context. Subjects perform, create, and interpret polyphonic, heteroglossic, and double-voiced dynamic texts that cannot be separated from ideological spheres, chronotopes, or horizons (worldviews). Bakhtin considers neither time nor the dialogic word as finite since their resonances increase in complexity and never end (Holquist 1981, 426–27). This echoes Peirce's notion of infinite regress. Indeed, Bakhtin sees the novel, like culture, as a process. Novelization becomes, in this sense, an apt metaphor for culture. Bakhtin's double voicing also characterizes language during communist periods, particularly that of the subjects under totalitarian Soviet rule. Poland developed a whole industry of exposing the double voicing of those who dared not directly say what they meant. And despite its often professed sincerity, the elite also spoke hypocritically.

The American ethnologists Tedlock and Mannheim, certainly taking their primary inspiration from Bakhtin, have designed a program of dialogic anthropology to supersede interpretative anthropology. However, as Tedlock and Mannheim show, dialogue had another advocate, Roman Jakobson, who as early as 1942 saw it as a more fundamental form of speech than monologue and called the latter a form of social pathology (Jakobson 1953a, 13 in Mannheim and Tedlock 1995, 1). Mannheim and Tedlock claim that "even as the voice of objectification or interpretation narrows itself toward an authoritative monologue," a multiplicity of voices goes suppressed (2–3). Thus dialogue for them, as for Jakobson and Lotman, includes internal dialogues. Accordingly, fieldworkers should never omit context, connotations, expressive features, or gestures when presenting native texts or interview transcripts since the many voices of these texts must remain in play. "The disciplinary voice of the ethnographer still has its place within a multivocal discourse, but this voice now becomes provisional," leaving room for the reader's interpretation (3). Performances communicate not only by verbal but also by nonverbal means such as rhythm, bodily movements, gazes, subtle moves, and through all the specifics of individual performers' characteristics such as power or histories of interaction (13).

As Bakhtin wrote:

> There are no "neutral" words or forms—words and forms that belong to "no one"; language has been completely taken over, shot through with intentions and accents. . . . Each word tastes of the context and contexts in which it has lived its socially charged life; all words and forms are populates by intentions. Contextual overtones . . . are inevitable in the word. (1981, 293)

> Heteroglossia, once incorporated into the novel, is *another's speech in another's language,* serving to express authorial intentions in a refracted way. Such speech constitutes a special type of *double-voiced discourse.* It serves two speakers at the same time and expresses simultaneously two different intentions: the direct intention of the character who is speaking, and the refracted intention of the author. In such discourse there are two voices, two meanings and two expressions . . . dialogically interrelated. (1981, 324)

Among the important themes that unite Bakhtin's position with ethnological studies are his carnival phenomena that act to erode boundaries and reverse hierarchies, carrying ideological implications by challenging official norms and canons and breaking down genres.

> Of the meaning and functions of worldwide images of the rogue, clown and fool—from the deep recesses of pre-class folklore up to the Renaissance— . . . we encounter new forms for making public all unofficial and forbidden spheres of human life, in particular the sphere of the sexual and of vital body functions (copulation, food, wine), as well as decoding of all the Symbols that had covered up these processes (common every-day Symbols, ritualistic ones and Symbols pertaining to the state religion). (Bakhtin 1981, 165)

As Bakhtin, Lotman, and Uspensky have noted, the dynamic role of laughter ranges from the sacred to the profane. In the medieval culture of Russia "some laughter images . . . bear no trace of ambivalence and do not lie outside the bounds of the official . . . culture" (Lotman and Uspensky

1984, 40), thereby resembling Turner's liminal world of reversals in initiation rites, where the grotesque remains within the sacred realm and where the official/nonofficial dichotomy ceased to exist. But in the world of the global village this may be history. Other studies of humor in tribal societies place laughter in the sacred realm (cf. Bricker's 1973 study of the highland Chiapas). Turner's liminoid in modern society (1982) recalls Bakhtin's carnival reversals of the social order in medieval Western society and, as in pre- and postcommunist Slovenia, humor no longer resides in the sacred realm. During the precommunist era carnival behavior of the liminoid type was not only celebrated at the traditional pre-Lent rituals in Žerovnica, but also was typically a part of festivities at intervillage markets and fairs. Villagers often nostalgically recalled these popular activities ruled out during the communist period. The ethnic community in Cleveland continued carnival celebrations not only as part of Catholic ritual but also in the farmlands outside of Cleveland where they included button box music, dramatic skits, dancing, beer, food. They were fully attended by all ages and accompanied by song, jokes, and humor.

Bakhtin's carnival minimally opposes and integrates two cultural worlds and their many internal divisions. Ethnic Slovene carnivalesque celebrations, such as the ones described above, equally stop or reverse time, transgressing cultural boundaries as ethnic Slovenes of all social classes join the feasting, dancing, and playing of traditional games. Old and young, men and women, suburbanites and inhabitants of traditional ethnic neighborhoods, ethnic language speakers and English speakers, churchgoers and secular individuals, all break down social restraints or underlying norms. The music of the button box player, who wears traditional costume, creates an agreement between heterogeneous objects emanating from different cultural systems. There are elements from the traditional culture, including the *balina* field, the linden tree (often seen as a marker of Slavic identity), Slovene food, drink, clothes, language, and gestures, all of them suggesting Lotman's implicit montage (the domain created being all that is village life in Slovenia). But if one focuses on juxtaposing these traditional activities and objects to features from the new culture, an example of explicit montage results.

Semiotics and Postmodern Studies: Their Interrelations and
Differences as Relevant to Ethnological Studies

Turning now to postmodern programs with no pretense for completeness,
it is clear that we are entering muddy waters: every aspect of what is considered to be modern from the Enlightenment on is now open to question.
What can we say that characterizes these diverse attitudes? At least for
ethnology the various versions of postmodernism inevitably bring to the
fore such controversial issues as, what is the relation of fact and theory? Can
we represent? Are there universals? Can we compare cultures or is each
culture unique? Is "adaptive" a sufficient rationalization for the diverse
practices that thwart comparison on any ethnical scale? Can history be
reduced to traces? Finally, we must ask what the interrelations between the
semiotic thinkers discussed are, and how they diverge from postmodern
positions.

The postmodern trend in ethnology has its beginning, some say, in the
sixties (Rabinow 1986). Postmodernism directs us to a questioning of ethnological methods, alerting ethnologists to the fact that they are writing
stories, that cultural behavior is a process of changing actions and that the
written narrative cannot directly mirror the raw data since it is infected with
the ethnologist's own perspective. Furthermore, the actors themselves do
not express a unitary point of view or voice, a notion akin to Bakhtin's
double voicing. Postmodernism shares the general disillusionment with the
modernist era, rationalism, optimism, and the belief in progress that has
dominated Western thinking since the Enlightenment. Thus representation,
if at all possible, certainly involves numerous limitations.

Some postmodernists reduce ethnographic depictions to mere construc-
tions and imaginative narrations, and consider the Enlightenment as totalitarian, reducing contextual issues to power plays. Such views point to many
of the glaring deficiencies and problems of the postindustrial age, and these
critiques cannot go ignored. However, one can criticize the reductionism,
oversimplification, and unadulterated relativism of some of the proponents
of the postmodern mood. Dreyfus and Rabinow, for example, reprimand
Bourdieu for not accounting for the "manifold significance of the practitioners" (1993, 41). In Bourdieu, they claim, the scientist understands the

meaning of human beings (maximizing Symbolic capital) while the practitioners are deluded. To them, this reductionist view does not then deal with the highly varied inventive and changeable cultural meanings of the actors. Such probing has been called "the hermeneutics of suspicion." As Ricoeur has written, one type of hermeneutics is animated by suspicion, skepticism, and distrust of the symbol. For him Marx, Nietzsche, and Freud are masters of suspicion. "All three aim to transcend this falsity through a reductive interpenetrating history" (1983, 6). As Dreyfus and Rabinow note, "The more common sense view denies that *all* action is motivated *solely* by the attempt to use the structure of the social field to increase Symbolic capital" (41). Furthermore, Bourdieu's notion that "a work of art is mainly of interest for someone who possesses . . . the code" because it otherwise appears as chaos without order (Bourdieu 1984, 2) recalls Saussure's position that a language arbitrarily imposes classification on a reality that is only a flux. On the contrary, the imposition of other codes onto a text by a non-member of the group is all too common, as when art objects from a formerly tribal culture hang on the halls of a modern Western museum.

Adorno's position that the Enlightenment is totalitarian is criticized by Docherty as a vast oversimplification (Adorno and Horkheimer 1986, 6 in Docherty 1994, 3). It is clear that fear of the power of the Enlightenment leads to the position that the Enlightenment controls all thinking. The Enlightenment is a specific form of reason reduced to mathematics, and much of reality is ruled out (Docherty 1994, 5–6). Baudrillard, perhaps the most important contemporary theorist of postmodernism, sees the bourgeoisie as disappearing and identities as "floating" modes of signification practices that radically depart from high modernity (Ashley 1990, 88). For Baudrillard the "social" is now unrepresentable: "In post-modern social formations, mass and media are indistinguishable; no distinction is made between simulation and representation of the mass" (Ashley 1990, 99 referring to Baudrillard 1983, 19). And, as Ashley continues, for Foucault "truth" is relative to the society or mode of domination (96, referring to Foucault 1980, 109–33).

Jameson, searching for some clues to unite or legitimize postmodernism, writes that postmodernism looks for breaks and for events. The modernism process is complete and nature has gone for good. "Postmodernism is the consumption of sheer commodification as a process" (1984, x). It is also the death of master "narratives" (xi).

The general questioning of traditional methodology has given rise to a radical reassessment of the writing of ethnology itself (cf. Clifford and Marcus 1986). Some go so far as to hold that ethnographic writing relies essentially on self-critical reflexivity, free-floating signifiers loosened from their signifieds, pastiche, tropes, heteroglossia, quotation, and traces. Important to postmodernists are the notions of metacommentary, allegory and irony, critiques of other ethnological writings, revised conceptions of the other as a dynamic part of the depiction, and avoidance of an absent ethereal voice and the reliance on rhetoric. Ethnological studies are seen as a kind of fiction or mere stories. Comparisons between cultures are not useful to postmodernist thinking since some find relativity so absolute that it amounts to incommensurability (cf. Clifford 1983, 1988). Some, like Tyler, even see ethnological writing as a kind of psychotherapy that helps the ethnologist to find himself. In addition, Tyler despairs of all writing and holds that ethnology is part of the humanities, not the sciences (1987).

Elsewhere, Marcus claims to be searching for new and immediate ways of contact and understanding (journalism is his preferred model here) (1993a, 1–16). He contrasts his suggestions with what he calls "text-based" practices of analysis (2, 3). Marcus believes that he is escaping textualization and finds that anthropologists' tendency to rely on "rational, detached reflective reason" hinders "more direct access to other's situated frameworks and discourses" (4).

I agree with Crapanzano's and Hammel's critiques of postmodernist views. Yet I find Hammel's rejection of postmodernism, which has led him to prophesize the death of anthropology, too pessimistic. While I regard postmodern positions as antitheoretical and antihistorical I do consider a call for fundamental changes in ethnological writings and for reevaluations of traditional official narratives necessary correctives to some extent. Yet I cannot accept the separation of the humanities from the sciences. Among other philosophers and anthropologists who reject this dichotomy are Holton, Margolis, Shattuk, Wolf, Hammel, and Crapanzano. Lévi-Strauss reminds us that these two ways of conceptualizing reality have never been isolated from each other and that contemporary science is overcoming the gap between humanities and sciences in its grasping of transformations of invariants (1963, 284).

Lévi-Strauss argues that histories may be viewed as the continuation of myths and that the open character of history is frequently secured by using and rearranging explanatory, originally mythical cells (40). He claims further that history often fulfills the function of myth to ensure that the future remains faithful to the present and the past (43). In this process myths, transformed and eventually exhausted, may be transferred into fictional elaborations or reactivations with a view of legitimizing history of either the retrospective type that founds a traditional order on the distant past, or of the prospective type that makes the past the beginning of the future. This position may be appropriated by official history or may legitimize nonofficial history, as I show in the next chapter on the history of Slovenia. Thus Lévi-Strauss emphasizes an "organic contiguity . . . among mythology, legendary history, and what we call politics" (1976, 268).

Crapanzano protests the postmodern stance. For him, the fate of the authoritative function presents a focal issue. He calls this function the Third, borrowing from Peirce a technically metapragmatic function that mediates any interlocution.

> It is symbolized . . . by such notions as the law, grammar, or tradition . . . by totems and fetishes. It may be embodied by father, king or priest . . . by spirits, deities and even by a third person (the audience) in any dyadic exchange. . . . When the Third is simply an empty function, there can be no communication. (1992c, 90)

This is clearly a Peircean interpretation of the unrestricted range of the Symbol which is never empty but based on reflection and relationships. Crapanzano also invokes Bakhtin's "double-voiced words." Given a strong commitment to the egalitarian pretense, no participant to the exchange may willingly admit that his recontextualizing response to the other has higher semantic authority, Crapanzano notes (1992c, 94). Such parodic situations portray present-day political discourse. Crapanzano ponders the fate of memory and history today, wondering whether this vacuum may not lead to defenselessness and even an attraction to fundamentalism (1992c, 99). He observes that the writing school of ethnography has created its own canon (1990, 303), for the dichotomy fiction/nonfiction is itself a historical and culturally specific opposition involving particular notions of narrative.

Theory and Fact

These arguments lead us to assess the relation of theory and fact. Jakobson's oft-repeated slogan "I hate theory without facts and facts without theory" has many implications. As Peirce has written, experience is our only teacher, and it is a validity that must be accounted for, but this is only part of the story.

In theory Peirce did not neglect the role of imagination, insight, and originality in all of his categories contributing to abduction. As he wrote, "Originality is the most primitive, simple and original of the categories" (CP 2.289); "all the ideas of science come to it by the ways of abduction" (CP 5.145). And:

> The abductive suggestion comes to us like a flash. It is an act of *insight,* although of extremely fallible insight. It is true that the different elements of hypothesis were in our minds before: but it is the idea of putting together what we have never before dreamed of putting together which flashes the new suggestion before our contemplation. (CP 5.128)

It follows from Peirce's view of abduction that

> the only hope of retroductive reasoning ever reaching the truth is that there may be some natural tendency toward an agreement between the ideas which suggest themselves to the human mind and those which are concerned in the laws of nature. (CP 1.12)

Jakobson also departed from the positivist requirements for establishing universals. He wrote,

> The frequent predilection for "absolute" exceptionless universals, as preferred to "near" universals, clashes once more with Sapir's warning against "the dogged acceptance of absolutes." Probability near to certainty but still less than 1.0 is as signal a phenomenon as probability 1.0. (1979, 237)

A far stricter test for truth is that of Karl Popper as reviewed by Holton:

> According to Popper we must subject our rational constructs to a curative purging regime so as to look for a fatal flaw even in our most treasured brain children. We must try hard to falsify, i.e., disprove them, and therefore to disown them. (1996, 97)

But, comments Holton somewhat in the spirit of Peirce,

> we must face the strange fact that there *are* genial spirits who can take the risk, and persevere for long periods without the comfort of confirmatory support, and survive to collect their prizes. (1996, 97)

Holton uses Isaac Newton, John Dalton, and Gregor Johann Mendel as examples (4). In a similar stance, Hillary Putnam notes that some philosophers, like Derrida, Goodman, and Rorty, "have reacted to the difficulty of our making sense of our cognitive relation to the world by denying that we do have a cognitive relation to extralinguistic reality" and he warns against throwing out the baby with the bath water (1992, xi).

I see the search for proof of the truth of semiotics of culture as grounded in a compromising solution that combines of Peirce, Jakobson, Holton, and Putnam. Their positions depart from the deconstructionists or postmodernists because they assert that we may hypothesize an outside reality. The semiotic scholars I have discussed would agree, I believe, that abduction or some similar method saves us from the unbridgeable chasm between fact and theory. Yet all theory is tentative and awaits further findings. Its value lies in its explanatory ability, its economy, and its avoidance of reduction and oversimplification.

Semiotics and Power

I conclude this primarily theoretical chapter, central to problems of interpreting culture texts, by touching upon one issue mentioned intermittently throughout this discussion, one which we must not marginalize—the role culture texts play in the game of power and domination. Contingent areas deploying power as a dominant mode may include culture texts expressing Bakhtin's official and nonofficial culture, Lotman's contrast in internal transfiguration, that is, Russians acting out the role of the French elite culture, the phenomenon of doublespeak, the role the elite in Žerovnica plays in the postcommunist years, who have been supported in the turn toward tourism, etc., and their implied meanings of power as opposed to the "others."

I turn here to Eric Wolf's suggestive deliberations in this domain. Attempting to explain the expanded interest in signs, he wrote that this concept had for some a way of making "the notorious and ambiguous concept of 'culture' more precise in semiotic terms," notably by drawing on Peirce as developed by Umberto Eco (1976, 67) who, Wolf held,

> took Peirce's relation to signs and relating it to the workings of culture accepting the fact that signs do not exist in reality, Eco pointed out that they depend for their formulation and function upon the network and communications we call culture. . . . Signs that assume the function of interpretants have a special role in the exercise of power because the capacity to assign cultural significance to signs constitutes an important role in domination. (1999, 54)

As Wolf points out (1999, 54–55), power for Parmentier (1994, 127–28) can determine the interpretants that will be admissible, emphasized, or expunged. According to Wolf, Bourdieu shows that language functions not only as an instrument of communication, but also as one of power (Wolf 1999, 55 referring to Thompson 1984, 46–47). Indeed, this pertains as much to visual as to audible signs and kinetic signs. In Žerovnica, the tax collector entering the village is a human sign of power. His uniform and authorative bearing sufficiently emphasize his authority. And when Mrs. Jaksic presides over a formal coffee hour in an elegantly furnished room in a house in the historic Slovene section of St. Clair Avenue in Cleveland, what does that mean for the ethnic Slovene from Žerovnica who fills the ambiguous role of servant/companion?

A world of signs of course has constantly embedded within it potential power functions, implicit or explicit, subtle or obvious. But we must avoid the trap of reducing signs to one function. I believe Wolf's conclusion is well-taken when he writes "that the human capacity to envision imaginary worlds seems to be shifting into high gear" (291). It is high time, then, for an investigation of how ideas, ideology, and power intermesh, and of how the many codes signify multiple messages implied or clear.

III

The Village and

the Slovene Communities

in Cleveland and Hibbing:

A Historical Perspective

Chapter Five

Žerovnica:

Its Past and the Question of Its Future

In this chapter I discuss the ethnographic materials pertaining to Žerovnica that I briefly surveyed in the introduction. I outline the main historical events both from the villagers' point of view and from the official record, and I include the community's perceptions of the future. Recollections, beliefs, tales, legends, myths, as well as childrens' autobiographies written in 1995–96 elucidate traditions, memories, and values of the past as they are challenged and change from the perspective of both youth and elders. I taped most of the tales and legends recited by a very old storyteller during early fieldwork in the village, republishing them here along with considerable data gathered in the eighties and nineties.

Language

I preface this section with a brief description of the Slovene language, which has a strong emotional hold over its speakers. It is one of the most archaic of Slavic languages and is rich in dialects and subdialects. The Slovene linguist Franc Ramovš has classified the dialect spoken in the area of Žerovnica and the Cerknica basin as a western subdialect of Lower Carinthian (*dolenjski dialekt*) (1931, 1957). It is bordered by the Inner Carinthian dialect (*notranjski dialekt*) spoken on the western side of the Javornik Mountains along the prewar Italo-Yugoslav border. To the north is the so-called *rovtarski* dialect. Morphologically and syntactically, the Žerovnica dialect does not deviate significantly from standard literary Slovene. The reduction of vowels, however, does differentiate its phonemic system. Thus, for example, *tukajle* (here) is pronounced "tle," and Martinjak (the name of the nearby village) is pronounced "Martnjak." Lexically, the Žerovnica dialect also distinguishes itself from standard literary Slovene by its large number of Germanisms (Ramovš 1933, 33). Migrants have gone to great efforts to preserve the language in the New World.

The Setting

In chapter 1 I have described the unusual setting of the village, whose limestone foundation constitutes the floor of two enclosed basins (*doline, polja*). The two most important are the Lož valley (*Loška dolina*) and the Cerknica basin in which Žerovnica is located (*Cerkniško polje*) about fifty kilometers southwest of Ljubljana. The two basins, separated by low hills, stretch from northwest to southeast, paralleling the Dinaric range. They are bordered on the southwest by the Javornik mountain range, rising to a height of 1,268 meters, which formed the Italo-Yugoslav border between the two world wars. In the northeast are the somewhat lower ranges of Menisija and Bloke, crowned by Mt. Slivnica (1,114m), an important landmark. To the south lies the highest range of the region, Mt. Snežnik (1,796m) as its peak. The southeastern tip of the Lož valley borders on Croatia.

The geological foundation of the karstic Cerknica lake, the shore of which abuts Žerovnica land, accounts for its seasonal drying and filling up. It is called *presihajoče jezero,* which literally means an intermittently drying out lake. Alluvial sediment covers its flat bottom. The geological foundation of the lake is filled by water from underground sources fed by nearby mountain streams as well as by small surface streams and rivers. In the summer the lake's water begins to disappear, emptying into the sink holes (*požiralniki*) in the karstic substructure.[1] At that time the lake bed is almost completely transformed into hay land, and only marsh grass and a small area of still water marks the lake. In early fall, rain water from the mountains replenishes the underground and surface waters, filling the lake more rapidly than the drainage holes can empty it.

At its lowest period the lake water covers half a square kilometer, while it floods twenty-five to twenty-six square kilometers, approximately half of the Cerknica *polje* at its southwestern end, at its highest. The hay land uncovered in late summer is mowed in August by all the villages surrounding the lake. Its hay, which the peasants call sour grass (*kisla trava*), is used for cattle bedding and only rarely for fodder. The northeastern parts of the *polje,* never flooded, provide excellent, fertile land. Once cattle also grazed on communal pastures at the edge of the lake lands, but most villages, including Žerovnica, have turned this desirable level land over to cultivation. Cattle, no longer numerous, are not let out to graze but are fed in their stalls. In the feudal era each villager was given one parcel of this fertile land laid bare when the lake recedes.

In the seventeenth century a Slovene nobleman, Johann W. Valvasor, described the lake in his now classical study of Slovenia (1686–89). Marveling at the lake's miraculous disappearance and its riches in fish and crabs, he wrote: "The Cerknica lake . . . can be called in all honor a rarity of all lakes, and a true wonder of nature. For this reason it has been classed as one of the most noble curiosities of waters by older and newer scribes through whose pens it has flowed" (4:619).

A UNESCO publication entitled *Cerkniško Jezero* (The Cerknica Lake) presents magnificent photographs and poetic descriptions of the lake (Peklaj, Kmelc, and Škoberne 1994). As the authors note, the historian Valvasor wrote down popular beliefs of his time, namely that the peak of the Slivnica mountain above Lake Cerknica was "a huge hollow, whence fairies and storms come." The lake was a place of miracles and magic steeped in legend. Both the Greek geographer Strabon and the Roman poet Virgil commented on it (1994, 8).

If one stands on the peak of the Slivnica Mountain, as I did, one looks down on a broad, strangely flat expanse of land, partially under water, the depression of the Cerknica *polje,* surrounded by steep slopes. The Cerknica basin below is crisscrossed by fields utilizing all the dry flat land surrounding the lake as well as that laid bare when the water recedes. Here one can observe the peasants' unique adaptation to the ecological situation. When the lake is dry, it becomes a source for hay, traditionally worked by peasants from all the villages abutting the lake. Today tractors, introduced only during the 1970s and 1980s, supplant ox-drawn equipment. The lake land lies to the west of Žerovnica, and mountains encircle most of the area. High on the *Križna gora* (Mountain of the Crosses) in the Bloke range, an old church becomes visible. It used to be the site of pilgrimages, but it is now in disuse except on a few Catholic holidays.

During the communist years, the vast fields to the northeast and east of the lake were owned by the Marof cooperative farm (*zadruga*), which was worked by tractors and combines.[2] Marof land met village lake lands to the south and northwest, and villagers, fearful that Marof might confiscate their lands and forests, regarded this proximity as ever-threatening. If one follows the neighboring narrower valleys through the mountains, the plain is soon lost from sight. More isolated, poorer mountain villages emerge here, places where sheep and cattle graze on high slopes and precipitously steep fields are worked by hand.

Traditionally, villagers have agreed that the lake is unconquerable and that no effort to interfere with its cycles would succeed. Ambitious plans to dry it up and expand arable land hence never came to realization. Indeed, it seemed that the lake had a kind of magical power. During haying, all who were able came out to the lake area with their wagons and oxen to reap the sour grass. Refreshing winds and the wide expanse of the basin rewarded them. A happy carnival atmosphere prevailed during the reaping, a marked change in mood since Žerovnica itself is very crowded and gives a rather somber impression.

In the past, until a road was constructed around the lake, timber cut from the hilly forest land was transported across the lake on rafts. Many nostalgically recall fishing expeditions and fantastic catches made possible when the lake receded in late summer.

In the village itself the houses are lined up facing each other, closely huddled together. Attached to the end of the homes are the barns for cattle and pigs that also house the *kuhinja,* the special stove for preparing feed for the pigs.[3] The air is filled with the scents of barnyards and family work in the kitchens and with the smell of animals.

The Historical Record, Legends, Tales, Myths
and Beliefs about the Past[4]

In the early Middle Ages the Slovenes came under the rule of German lords and the Catholic Church. In the thirteenth and fourteenth centuries most Slovene land had become part of the Hapsburg feudal domain. The Yugoslav kingdom's establishment ended this rule in 1918. A brief Turkish invasion in 1492 had not left a strong mark, but the history of the village burning by the Turks was recounted by an elder villager, a former itinerant musician and singer at weddings, who was the source of many folk tales.

In the old days the Turks came to Žerovnica. Everyone fled and took their cattle with them. But in one house an old woman was left. She heated a pot and put everything evil-smelling into it, bones, manure, and so forth. The people said they could smell it for half an hour's walk away. So the Turks did not enter the village. They came to another forest and another village and they burnt it down. This is why Žerovnica was saved.

The feudal period was marked by unrest. The empress Maria Theresa (1717–80) and her son Joseph II (1765–90) responded to peasant protest with an enlightened policy of agrarian reform that alleviated feudal burdens. During Napoleon's short incursion from 1809 to 1813 Napoleon Carniola was incorporated into the Illyrian province, with Ljubljana as its capital.

The Origin of the Lake and Related Tales

The traditional teller of tales and button box player who described the Turkish incursions also related the story of the origin of the lake which is attributed to the miraculous action of a young prince of Šteberk who lived in the ancient castle. At that time, as the legend has it, a bog, studded with oaks and other trees, covered the area that is today under water. In the most frequent version told in the village, the narrator recounts the following story related to him, he says, by a friend as they went boating on the lake:

> When I was young, I used to go boating on the lake. Well, almost our entire village went there once. And we were sitting in the boat talking about all sorts of things. Then one spoke, and said: "That is nothing, I heard how this lake came to be." "Well, then, tell us," I said. And he began to tell us. He was a carpenter, a small little man, and a hunchback. "Well," he said, "where now the Karlovica [one of the main sink holes of the lake] is, there stood a castle—there is still a small section of the wall there. [The Šteberk castle and the Karlovica sink hole are on opposite sides of the lake]. We own a small forest right by that castle, below and above it. And there is also a cellar there, a big one—I do not know what they used it for. During the war, the second one, the partisans hid in that cellar—they had benches and a stove in there so they could warm themselves.
>
> "When the young prince of Šterberk was the master, there was a girl at the Karlovica, the poor girl. That prince wooed her, but the count at Karlovica,

her father, refused to give up his daughter. He told the young prince, 'Only if you come for her in a boat can you have her.' And the young prince felt a premonition of something terrible. He went riding—he had a beautiful white horse. And a man appeared from a valley and said, 'Why are you so sad?' 'How can I help it,' said he. 'There is a girl I would like to marry, but her father will not allow it. Only if I come for her in a boat may I have her. How can I do this? What should I do?' and that man said, 'I shall tell you what to do. Cover a drainage hole with a grid, make strong iron grids, and put a lot of dirt over them, and when it rains a lake will form.' And he did so. It began to rain, and the lake appeared. Then he made a large boat, and sailed across. And truly, the father was not happy at all—but he had given his word and he had to keep it. The boy and the girl agreed that she would set a light for him in the evening. And he used that light as a guide and came to see her every evening. But suddenly others came from elsewhere to ask for the girl's hand. And her father was glad—but the girl was not. She said, 'I have my man—he comes to me every evening—I just set the light on the window for him and he comes on the boat.' But the father plotted with one of her suitors, or he bribed one of the maids, to carry the light over to the Karlovica. The young man from Šteberk followed the light and came to the Karlovica. The water swallowed him—the boat was so big and listing so heavily that its name was visible on its side. The girl was looking for the young man, wondering why he had not come. She looked at the window—there was no light. She walked around the castle and glanced at the Karlovica—the light was still burning there in the daylight. And she saw the boat—its name was there as before. She said, 'Someone set the light there on purpose,' and she also threw herself into the water. And so then there was the lake. No one could reopen the hole—and this is how the lake came to be." (Portis-Winner 1971, 38–40)

Thus ends a folk version of the Romeo and Juliet myth.

Other folk tales recounted by villagers describe the autocratic rule of the count. It is said that the people were not allowed to fish in the lake except when a bell rang in Cerknica. But no sooner had the villagers caught their fish than the count would rule that all the fish were for the castle. The people would then throw the fish back into the lake as the count cursed them, saying, "Death to all" (39).

Another tale ridicules the countess:

Once the peasants were mowing on all sides. There was the corvée then, and the peasants went up there to mow. Well, the countess came to take a little walk, to cool off a little. She had a parasol and watched the peasants mowing. When they stopped to sharpen their blades, she said, "Do not scritch scratch, finish the job" ("*Nix figl-fajgl, durch mahaj*").[5] The mowing went so slowly with dull blades that finally the countess said, "First scritch scratch, then finish!" (39)

Witches also appear in the early tales. One story describes the burning of a village to rid it of a witch (*copernica*). On a map drawn by Valvasor around 1686, the top of Mt. Slivnica is labeled as a gathering place for witches (*Hexenzusammenkunft*). Under the Count of Šteberk, it is said, witches were tortured, the gallows were busy, and peasants were beaten. Excerpts from the following early tale recounted to us by an old village woman demonstrate these beliefs:

Šteberk castle ruled all these villages. They were all raising cattle for him up there, all these villagers. And they say there also were large prison cells in the castle. If someone disobeyed and was not submissive, they would throw him into that prison. In those earlier times, people believed strongly in witches. If a woman was accused of being a witch, they would chain her and chase her from the castle through Žerovnica to Grahovo, and then to Martinjak. Then the hangman would take her and close the gates where the big gallows were. While they chased a witch, all the church bells would toll for her last hour. Saint Pavel, here in our village, and Mary of the Immaculate Conception in Grahovo, it is called so, and in Martinjak there is another church, it was called St. Leo. St. Leo would toll till the end, until she was hung. And if she cried out on her way—they cut off her tongue. There, where they were catching fish down in the lake and along those shores, there was a guard, or a policeman, with a whip. If someone did not want to catch fish, he would beat him on the naked back. He would let him have it with a real whip, they say.

Our teller of tales described feudal oppression. Here is an example:

Each peasant also had to work for the count for fourteen days. Then the local count—that old one—died and they brought one of his relatives from Germany, but again it did not work out and that one also left. Then all fell into decay. Now, at Saint Ann, up there on the top, they have found the cemetery of these counts. And they found a skeleton there; it is now some two or three years since—and there were golden chains and golden rings on the skeleton, which was still intact. And it is perhaps two, three, or four hundred years old, or even older. Well, the castle came to be. And then, after it fell apart, it was no more.

The Origin of the Village and the Developing Economy
and Social Structure

The former village head (*podžupan*), the keeper of records and a natural historian, related data to show that there were twelve founding families occupying the center of the village, each holding one full *zemlja* including hay land, forest land, and perhaps two-and-one-half hectares of plow land. Pasture land was held in common. Inheritance was joint, that is shared by all sons. In other words, the village shared in the tradition of the South Slavic *zadruga*. Mosely's definition gives the minimal characteristics of the *zadruga*:

> A household composed of two or more biological or small families, closely related by blood or adoption, owning its means of production communally, producing and consuming the means of its livelihood jointly, and regulating the control of its property, labor, and livelihood communally. (1940, 95; cf. Portis-Winner 1971, 73–82 and 1977a for a full discussion of the issue of the early joint family or *zadruga* in Slovenia)

I have reconstructed the narrative line of the story based on information, maps, and records from the former village *podžupan*, Matija Rok, and widespread village beliefs as follows.

Žerovnica was established in the dim past by twelve founding families or their descendants that became subject to the rule of the overlord. These land holdings had been established, it is said, when each of the seven large complexes of communal, cultivable village land were divided into twelve equal parts, thus facilitating a villagewide crop rotation system (*kolobar-jenje*) in which each of the twelve families held one *zemlja* composed of seven separate fields, one in each complex. In the next epoch, according to legend, family lands began to be divided equally among brothers, and all sons, except the oldest who inherited the father's house, built their new houses close by on the family land. Finally, the legend refers to a recent period, approximately three or four hundred years ago, when most *gos-podars* (family heads) owned only one quarter *zemlja*, equal division was halted, and land scarcity required the adoption of the principle of impar-tibility and primogeniture. Since then younger sons were expected to seek their livelihood elsewhere or find a supplementary village occupation.

Matija Rok, the former
village headman

The strength of this narrative demonstrates that we cannot ignore the
viability of memories. As Evans-Pritchard wrote, "A people's traditional
history . . . forms part of the thought of living men and hence part of the
social life which the anthropologist can directly observe" (1961, 6). The
wider historical context, the traditions of the early civilizations of Indo-
European and Semitic peoples that also imparted the number twelve with
special significance, suggests that the narrative at one time had sacred as
well as social meaning.[6] From the twelve Greek gods to the twelve founding
tribes of Israel fathered by Jacob and the twelve apostles, themes parallel to
our story find expression. As Guthrie writes: "Mainly out of Homer, and
certainly in Ionia at an early date, there took shape the circle of the Twelve
Gods, which formed a kind of canon for the Greeks of succeeding centuries" (1955, 35). Under the aegis of Zeus, Guthrie comments, the family of
gods, modeled on a human clan, eventually settled on Mount Olympus (37).
Guthrie offers various evidences that the twelve gods were conceived as a
kind of corporate body in classical times. There is the altar to the Twelve at

Athens, the oath "by the Twelve" in Aristophanes, their association with the zodiac and various treatments of the Twelve by Greek classical writers, architects, and sculptors. As Guthrie concludes:

> It is clear that the corporate conceptions of the Twelve retained its signifi-cance throughout and beyond the classical period, so that this collective expression called forth definite associations in the mind of a Greek. With Zeus at their head and the clearly marked character which each possessed, they doubtlessly represented between them . . . all that was most typical in Hellenic religious, political and social ideas. . . . To mark his companion-ship of Hellenic ideals, Alexander built an altar to the Twelve in India. . . . The compactness and the definite character of the Twelve probably had its origin in the conscious work of archaic priests and legislators. (35)

Even as far distant as Senapur in North Central India does an origin tale exist that has important parallels to that of Žerovnica. It also dramatizes the symbolism of "twelve" (Opler and Singh 1948, 464–69). One is reminded of Maine's observation that while India and Europe had different climates and consequently different systems of agriculture, the early village communities were similar in that they upheld

> rules which in both cases have the same object—to reconcile a common plan and order of cultivation on the part of the whole brotherhood with the holding of different lots in the arable land by separate families. (1876, 109)

In Senapur, according to Opler and Singh, the landlord caste believed itself descended from one of the twelve grandsons of an early pioneer. Among the twelve, the land was divided equally and identification with the grandsons remained a basis for property classification, for participation in the local political and administrative structure, and for the recruitment of leaders. Similarly, in Žerovnica those who believed themselves descended from one of the twelve founders held larger land holdings and formed a traditional elite.

The legendary reconstruction of the early social organization and inheri-tance customs of Žerovnica raises a controversial issue. What is the position in early society of the traditional South Slavic *zadruga,* or joint family, a basic rural institution that persisted in all South Slavic countries except Slo-venia until the nineteenth century? Scholars do not agree on this issue and cite various kinds of evidence to support their conclusions. While Moseley held Slovene society held no evidence of an early *zadruga* (1953, 222), the Slovene scholars Melik (1963), Vilfan (1961), and Kos (1955) generally believe in its existence, primarily based on linguistic evidence (cf. Portis-Winner 1971, 59–64). While I noted signs of tension between brothers over inheritance rules during my stays in Žerovnica, the loyalty to brothers and to family was strongly evidenced by the remittances sent home from the ethnic Slovenes in America.

Historical Events from 1848 to the Communist Period

When Austrian decrees of 1848 and 1849 ended tithes and the corvée, most of the agricultural land in Slovenia was in peasant hands. During this period peasant poverty increased, forcing villagers to find ingenious ways to survive. One source was lumber. The forest has always been Slovenia's greatest source of natural wealth. Peasants look on their forest land as a gold reserve, permanently available when a family is threatened with heavy taxes or unpredictable emergencies such as crop failure or illness.

In 1857 a railway line was opened from Ljubljana to Trieste, making the nearby town of Rakek a major station for wood loading, thus destroying the peasant carting trade along this route. Villagers began to cart lumber for local landowners from the Lož valley, about five miles from Žerovnica, to Rakek—an occupation that became the main source of outside income until after World War II. Horse smuggling (*tihotapstvo*) was a popular source of income for peasants from the Lož valley to Cerknica throughout the interwar period. Villagers could buy horses in Croatia and move them through the forest to Italy, where they were sold for twice their original price. This now romanticized activity is the subject of a popular 1964 novel entitled *The Smugglers* (*Tihotapci*) by M. Hace, a former partisan. Women smuggled meat, butter, and eggs in exchange for Italian rice and saccharine, both of which brought good prices back home.

Cattle trading was a central activity in the earlier village. Villagers recall that markets (*sejem*) were held six times a year on the Žerovnica church hill, providing opportunities for daylong fairs and general celebrations, gambling, clown performances, and feasting. Other social activities included carnival (*pust*), the traditional *kolina,* and celebrations on religious holidays.

The villagers associated life under the Austrian monarchy and the kingdom of Yugoslavia between the two world wars with some positive aspects in spite of persistent poverty, low-level farming technology, and increasing taxes. Peasants report visiting, wedding celebrations lasting as long as three days, choral group performances, plays put on by the village firemen's association (*gasilno društvo*). All such celebratory performances were ruled out during the communist period. Peasants insisted that under communism they had no time to visit each other and time became a scarce commodity.

Due to growing poverty and pressure on limited land resources during the agrarian crisis of the 1890s, large-scale emigration of Slovenes to the United States began. Villagers report that members of the ethnic community supported their village families since the 1890s. This was no longer imperative in the postcommunist village although the elders are the poorest group and do receive some aid from their children who often reside in Ljubljana or other industrial centers. Yet despite growing independence of the youth no family felt itself complete without taking account its absent members whose visits they frequently described and whose photos and mementos adorned the main room (*hiša*) of the house. Not until recently did reports from visiting ethnic Slovenes or in newspapers shatter the comforting belief in the American dream. Although the early immigrants faced the realities of gaining a living in a new country whose language they did not know and where they often had to take positions for unskilled workers, their stubbornness and pride often kept them from communicating negative news to the families at home.

In spite of the remittances from departed relatives, financial need in Žerovnica grew during the worldwide economic crisis of the 1920s and 1930s. Medium-sized landowners and poor peasants suffered particularly severely. Following are some typical stories about the depression years. The widow of a peasant who owned a quarter *zemlja* told of her family's experience:

> My husband went to America at seventeen (in 1906) and stayed until the First World War. He worked with a relative in the mines of Minnesota. He went because his father's farm was terribly in debt. There were six children, and my husband's father had to send his son to America. My husband said to his mother before he left, "If I earn 1,000 *forints* can I come home?" She said, "You earn that much and you will be master in this house." If it had not been for earning in America this farm would have disappeared. My husband came

home and fixed up the house with the money he made from America. (Portis-Winner 1971, 88)

The son of a village specialist, who also resorted to emigration, told his own story.

My father was a shoemaker and had five children. He had only one field of potatoes. In the 1880s he went to Pennsylvania. Then he went to Brazil. I went to America also, but my father got sick in Brazil and returned to the village, so I came back to help him. Then my father died, so I went back to America and sent money to my mother and brothers and sisters. I worked in the mines in Minnesota. In 1914 I came back to the village, but the rest of my brothers remained in America. Then I was able to buy a little more land. But I should have stayed in Minnesota for another ten years. I came back because my mother needed me, and then I had to go to war. (88)

The son of an impoverished quarter-*zemljak,* who had lost some land in the late nineteenth century and had emigrated to France, related this story:

My father called me home in 1931. The house was deeply in debt. I said, "What will be, will be" (*"kar bo bo"*). Either it will be sold or it will stay. When I came back, it was very bad here. It was a lucky house that had one hundred dinars in cash. I sold wood for seventy-five dinars a cubic meter. There was no trade, nothing. No one could pay taxes. The government just waited for years and years but did not take anything. (88)

Another view stresses individual pride and initiative, and the protective role of the traditional social fabric. A well-to-do peasant, who owned a half *zemlja,* held that no villager was ever allowed to starve and that the village council always provided for those in want; those in need were fed by various houses in turn. He recalled that when a poor woman who was married to a charcoal maker and lived in a lean-to in the Žerovnica woods turned to drink and moved away leaving her child, the village cared for the child since it had been born in Žerovnica.

Austrian rule in the area that is now Slovenia came to an end in 1918 with the establishment of the Yugoslav Federation. The new South Slav state (Slovenes, Croats, and Serbs), later renamed Yugoslavia (Jugoslavija; *jug* means south in Serbo-Croatian and Slovene) was at first called the Kingdom of the Serbs, Croats, and Slovenes. The province of Slovenia included most of the former Austrian territories inhabited by the Slovenes: the former duchy of Carniola (German: *Krain*, Slovene: *Kranj*), a considerable section of Styria (German: *Steiermark*, Slovene: *Štajersko*), and a small section of Carinthia (German: *Kärnten*, Slovene: *Koroško*). The Yugoslav constitution of 1922, which supported Serbian centralism and democratic forms, ended with the establishment of a royal dictatorship in 1929. After the assassination of King Alexander I in 1934, however, a milder autocratic government continued its rule until World War II. Yet conditions for the peasants did not improve.

World War II and the Communist Decades

On March 24, 1941, Yugoslavia signed the Tripartite Pact, and two days later the pro-German Yugoslav government fell. On April 2 the Germans invaded Yugoslavia, and after twelve days the Yugoslav army capitulated. This period also saw the beginning of the resistance, which grew to such strength that the greater part of the Yugoslav countryside remained under guerrilla control throughout the war. In 1941 the Italians occupied the Cerknica area, and in 1942 one villager was executed. The Italians shelled the village in May 1941, setting ten houses on fire. By July 1942, forty to fifty inhabitants of Žerovnica aged 16 to 60 had been transported to a concentration camp on the island of Rab.

The year 1945 saw the establishment of communist rule, and Slovenia became a part of the Federative Socialist Peoples' Republic of Yugoslavia, and remained a part of the federation until Slovenia achieved independence after a one-week war in 1991. Slovenia then received international recognition and an independent Slovene state was established on January 12, 1992.

I briefly described the negative aspects of the communist decades in chapter 1, and we have noted the nostalgic recollections of lost social, cultural, and economic activities of all kinds, including the thrill of smuggling, under the communist regime. Indeed, the disappearance of village-wide activities, the loss of free markets for agricultural and animal products and lumber, the prices of which were now controlled by the neighboring cooperative farm Marof and the nearby furniture factory Brest, were all severe shocks to the village economy and way of life. All but one of the four mills were shut down, and the one remaining was subject to severe restrictions. A small new village elite grew. It was composed of *gospodars* who participated in the socialist enterprises and bureaucracy of the government, the cooperative farm Marof, the factory Brest, or the *občina* administration in Cerknica.

While the post-1848 village had a measure of local political autonomy and was governed by an elected village council under the village head (*podžupan*), this partial autonomy was lost under the hierarchical communist regime. Peasants, heavily taxed, frequently found themselves in debt. Ironically, the village survived and produced its products, while, by the end of the communist years, the Marof cooperative farm had gone bankrupt and was reduced to raising chickens and selling the eggs. Villagers frequently remarked that "the peasant works only for taxes," and the only solution during the years of Tito's rule had been to combine factory work with Brest in Martinjak, reachable by bicycle or moped, with agricultural work. Brest went bankrupt in Martinjak but survived in Cerknica. Most families had at least one member working in the factory at one time. Although factory labor added to the family income, it also placed a heavy burden on the peasant family that no longer had many children and was thus left shorthanded in the fields.

The juridical settlement of disputes further eroded village autonomy. Traditionally the village council or local court had settled conflicts between villages over such issues as boundaries, inheritance, rights to forest land, and road construction. But government officials took on these tasks under the communist regime.

The Catholic Church lost most of its power, and the village lost its priest. Mass was held only in the parish house in nearby Grahovo. And the dwindling male village choir performed only infrequently at the church in Cerknica. Priests attempted to continue to offer their services, and Catholicism remained a strong moral force, but attendance at masses declined and often civil authorities carried out marriage ceremonies while religious ceremonies were held only surreptitiously.

There was little time or enthusiasm during the communist years for such traditional arts as public decorative painting, the carving of religious motifs, or basketry. Markets, carnivals, and three-day weddings also seemed to disappear from everyday life. One still saw colorful tile stoves, wall stippling giving the impression of wallpaper, woven cloths, wooden carvings on boxes, and simple handcarved furniture inside the peasant houses. But local folk art declined during the communist period, becoming commercialized and standardized. Kitsch items were sold in state-controlled tourist stores.

In general, one can conclude that the communist years were a time of cultural impoverishment for the village and that villagers did not benefit from land or other reforms. High taxation continued. At best we can say that some of the most unpopular policies were abrogated after 1948 when Tito broke with the Cominform. Attempts at enforced collectivization, which peasants in Yugoslavia generally, and particularly in Žerovnica, refused, were abandoned in 1953, as were fixed quotas of agricultural products that the peasants were required to deliver to the state. The adoption of the communal administration system in Yugoslavia in 1955 gave the village some limited rights to participate in its own government, but these were essentially nominal. In general, peasants saw themselves as the least protected sector of society and as the lowest echelon on the status ladder, hardly appreciated for their important contribution to the Yugoslav economy.

The Postcommunist Village

In the years following Slovenia's independence, the village became more heterogeneous and strangely different. Fewer children and young people were visible. Some houses were deserted, and the upkeep of the village had deteriorated. Home owners no longer kept their fenced front gardens uniformly well. On the other hand, there were at least two houses under major reconstruction. I soon learned that these houses represented a key to the future goals of the village. *Občina* officials and those middle-aged villagers who, having had somewhat better jobs than factory work, were well off and had the right connections with the *občina*. Some received loans from the *občina* to convert, under strict regulations, their houses to bed-and-breakfasts. These strict restoration regulations were meant to preserve the outward symmetry of the village (cf. *Ljubljanski regionalni zavod* 1985). Economic differences, however, were greater than ever. The fields were not fully cultivated, and frictions were now becoming more obvious between those able to finance changes for tourism and the many others who could not. There was evidence of modernization: tractors, refrigerators, televisions, automobiles, telephones, and modern plumbing had become very common.

Our old friends greeted us with excitement, hospitality, and food. In the house in Grahovo where we had lived with our children during the early study, the baby, Meta Polovič, was now a young married schoolteacher with a son, Simon. Meta became my assistant.[7] Her grandmother, Marija (Micka) Mertelj, who very warmly received us on our first return in 1992, and who grew up in Žerovnica, had died by the time of our second visit in 1995. The house of the former Žerovnica *podžupan* Matija Rok and his wife Marija, both of whom died before our return, was now left to their daughter, Marija, and son-in-law, Anton (Tone) Primožič, while their now grown daughters, Marija and Tončka (Antonia), worked in Ljubljana. The new *gospodar* and *gospodinja* who greeted us enthusiastically looked tired and somewhat abandoned. Except on weekends, they were left alone to do the farm work.

Clearly, surface impressions hinted at some fundamental changes concerning the economy and associated interpersonal relations, and the move toward tourism, and the relations with relatives in Cleveland and Hibbing. For the younger generation, nostalgia for the past was supplemented with ambitions to join the modern world.

The Economy

A disaffected youth, many of whom had received some professional training and had found employment in Ljubljana and other towns, constituted an overwhelming problem for older peasants. The younger generation does, however, try to return for weekends and maintain a strong attachment to the village, helping with farm work when at home, but this does not significantly help the parents' labor. One villager who works the land full-time told us that his income was so low that he would have been better off if he had just taken a pension. But he was used to working on the land and wanted to continue nevertheless.

Most villagers agreed that the economic situation had improved for some, but that it still was necessary to combine farming with factory work when possible. Yet by and large villagers complained that the peasant was still the most exploited member of society. Villagers frequently lamented others' unfriendliness and complained that houses stood too close to each other—a marked contrast to the repeated phrase we heard during our previous visits: "We are a friendly village and all have an equal amount of land." The large differential between the low prices they received for their products and the high cost of equipment and supplies such as tractors, fuel, and fertilizer strained the peasant household. The age-old crop rotation scheme (*kolobarjenje*) had been abandoned, and most villagers now limited their crops to potatoes and fodder for their animals. Yet land plots had not undergone redistribution. Some families, as for instance the Primožič family, grew their own food, baked their own bread, and used only natural fertilizer. Since the fall of communism, villagers have sold their lumber to private mills in Cerknica and Logatec and their milk to a creamery in Cerknica that has not yet been privatized. However, the Slovene economy suffered greatly, since independence brought with it the loss of principal markets in the other republics of the old Yugoslav federation largely because of the effects of the Bosnian war and the strife in Kosovo. In addition, there is some unemployment now. It is for this reason that emigration, primarily to the United States, Canada, and Australia is continuing, even if on a smaller scale than in earlier years.

Many villagers deplore the continued economic exploitation of the peasants and assert that consumers did not appreciate the peasants' labor. They resent the large discrepancies between the original sale and the resell price the creamery imposes on their milk. They complain that the buyer then skims some of the cream off the top and sells the milk as "whole milk" to the stores, although the fat content is only 2.5–3 percent instead of the 4 percent of genuine whole milk. We heard the same complaint about prices paid by the middleman to the peasant for potatoes and other products. Families complained about high unemployment, even though official reports indicated that only some 100,000 individuals were out of work in Slovenia in 1995, a number that constitutes approximately 1.8 percent.

In some ways the security of the peasants had begun to improve even before independence and the fall of communism. Until the 1970s, villagers not also employed in a state enterprise could not buy old-age and disability insurance. This changed in 1974, but a general feeling of insecurity remained. On being asked about this, Tone Primožič said: "Our situation is okay as long as I am healthy. But if I am no longer well enough to work the

Field work

fields, then it is not so good." This general concern about the future is not only based on insufficient insurance, but also on the shortage of family workers. While most families today have to rely on only one generation to work the fields, two or sometimes even three generations performed this task together in the 1960s and 1970s.

The village has received modern improvements. There is now an ambulatory clinic in Cerknica. There is a small private stand-up restaurant (*bife*). Power saws are now used for felling trees, and some of the mills use electricity instead of water power. The most striking changes in the village are the private stores that have sprung up, offering a great variety of goods. In the 1960s and 1970s, the peasants were obliged to go to Cerknica, Postonjna, or Ljubljana for many of the things now sold privately, since there was only a small general store in nearby Grahovo. Now the village has a grocery and even a hardware store that sells all types of building materials such as bricks, tile, lime, cement, iron frame mesh, windows, doors, plumbing, and electric materials.

Tourism and Impressions of America

The most important element reflecting the new life in the village are the preparations for establishing the area of the Cerknica Lake as a tourist center. This tourist activity favors Žerovnica as the sole typical traditional

TOURIST FARM

Ivanka and Jože Logar

Žerovnica 16, 61384 GRAHOVO
SLOVENIA
TEL.: +386/61 79 20 71

A flier advertising the remaking of Žerovnica as a tourist village. Žerovnica's oldest structure serves as its logo.

The village of Žerovnica lies on the eastern fringe of Lake Cerknica. Through the village runs the Žerovnčica stream, where there used to be five mills for grinding flour and sawmills, some of them are still in operation. The village rises gently towards a hill dominated by a lovely little church. At the foot of the hill stands an old granary, the focal points of the village's special pattern. The village with the granary is protected as part of the national cultural heritage.

The farm welcomes all visitors and offers a wide range of products: home-made sausages and other typical meat products, dried fruit (apples, prunes), strawberries, apple vinegar, home-brewed brandy, bread baked in the oven of the farm's range, as well as a variety of pastry (also on order).
If you want to have a warm lunch or diner, we offer you Nortranjska regional specialties prepared on the basis of our own farm products.
Those interested in gardening can have a look at the old orchard with medium large trees and species of old fruit-trees, as well as our intensive strawberry production.
On warm spring days you can borrow a bike for a nice ride in the wonderful countryside or simply go for a walk in the mountains of Križna gora and Slivnica, or to the Križna jama cave, a typical example of karst underground formations and a site where cave bear skeletons were found.
We can also arrange a ride for you in an open carriage to Snežnik Castle or around Lake Cerknica-the jewel of our valley.
As of summer 1995 you will be able to stay in the first-class apartments at the farm's old homestead (half board, full board).
This description comprises only a part of the farm's offer;

let your curiosity lead you to us, and see it for yourselves!

Distances:			
By car:		On foot:	
Ljubljana (by motorway)	45 mins	Lake Cerknica	15 mins
Italy (by motorway)	45 mins	Križna gora	45 mins
the Bloke plateau	15 mins	Križna jama	40 mins
Snežnik Castle	15 mins	Slivnica	60 mins

WELCOME TO THE LOGAR FAMILY FARM!

road village left in Slovenia. Additional advantages stem from the surrounding area, the natural wonder of the ever-changing lake, and the abundance of karstic caves that, it is hoped, will attract tourists.

The new plans for tourism have brought with them the concept of the "tourist farm" (*turistična kmetija*). Participants in the new move, those with contacts to the *občina*, are beginning to compose a new village elite. Considerable animosity has developed between these "haves" and the other "have nots." The Logar family, for example, had been presented with a second house in the village by a relative who had emigrated to Australia. This enabled them to move to that house, tear down their old house, and erect an entirely new building on the old foundation. They then moved back to the newly constructed house in which, as they said, "even the spoons were new." They are now remodeling their second house as a bed-and-breakfast. *Občina* funds underwrote both the rebuilding of the original house and the adaptation of the new house for tourism. Other families are following this example. For instance, the *občina* has been aiding a family with subsidies at low interest rates. Having renovated the second floor according to urban standards, the young family plans to move to nearby Cerknica and rent out their top floor in Žerovnica to tourists. The elders will continue to inhabit the unchanged ground floor, a fact which seems to leave them lonely and dispirited.

The owners going into the tourist business told us that they greatly prefer Slovenia to America because of the lack of sufficient social security in the United States. This attitude differed sharply from the earlier belief in the American dream.

The Law for the Protection of National Monuments (Zakon o naravni in kulturni dediščini), promulgated in 1981 (cf. Zakon 1981), has established a Monument Protection Agency (Ljubljanski regionalni zavod az varstvo naravne in kulturne dediščine) whose principal task it is to supervise new construction in the village. For Žerovnica this law means that no new structures can be added to the village, although building on old foundations, as in the case of the Logar family, is permitted, albeit under the strict supervision of the Protection Agency and in accordance with specific rules for Žerovnica, which require that the front of the house must face the street like all houses now do, prescribes the pitch of the roof and the color of its roof tiles, the position of windows and outside doors, as well as ornamentation. The law prohibits the erection of new buildings in the village proper, although building at the periphery is allowed. These restrictions and regulations aim to preserve the traditional look of the village. The owners of the newly to be established "tourist farms," we were told, must pass a cooking examination in the preparation of typical peasant food.

In 1993, a Society of Tourist Guides for Notranjsko was formed to assure better service for tourists. The society developed a set of rules and a plan to increase the quality and ecological acceptability of tourism in the Cerknica *občina*, and for the training of local guides. The first important tourist event was the "Valvasor Promenade," organized for June 26, 1993 to commemorate the three-hundredth anniversary of Valvasor's death. The purpose of this promenade, we were told, was to show the beauty of the lake, which would appeal to all kinds of tourist groups: peasants, fishermen, bird-watchers, and simply tourists. The promenade included a visit to the only island village in Slovenia, Otok, in the middle of the Cerknica Lake, and all the villages surrounding the lake. Visitors were able to inspect a mechanical model of the valley, the Cerknica Lake, and the western edge of the Javornik, Slivnica, and Križna Gora Mountains located in the village Dolenja vas. The model, located in a small room attached to a private buffet, is owned by Viktor Kebe who demonstrates it to tourists. The initiator and creator of the model is the academic artist Milan Rot. We were given a private showing of the relief model, and in the space of half an hour we were able to see the lake in all its stages: from a dry field to a lake full of water and overflow back to a dry field.

Plans to establish the Notranjsko Regional Park (Notranjski regijski park) in an area of 1,627 square kilometers, which will include the districts of Ilirska Bistrica, Postojna, Cerknica, and Logatec, make for another innovation inspired by tourism. The protected areas in this park will cover an area of 600 square kilometers and will include the Cerknica Lake, the Planina field, the Postojna karstic caves, Mt. Snežnik, and from there back in the direction of Cerknica. The project's purpose is to protect the biological varieties of life, the natural development, and the human culture of the region. Authorities hope that such an ecologically controlled form of tourism will provide a new chance at a better life for the inhabitants of the region. The plan requires the construction of hotels and inns for the accommodation of tourists. At the moment, the only tourist rooms in the Cerknica area are in Rakov Škocjan, which offers simple facilities for only twenty guests. The official history and future of building tourism does not take note of the situation of many peasants, particularly the older ones, who cannot participate in this endeavor.

Ambitions and Nostalgia: Autobiographies and Impressions
of the Young in Independent Slovenia

What follows are four examples of the thirteen written autobiographies by schoolchildren and young adults collected by my assistant, Meta Polovič, in 1995. Meta's own comments, which attempt to isolate main themes, form the conclusion.

The first autobiography cited is by a young adult woman, Andreja Godeša, born in 1973. It was the only autobiography written in English.

> I was very surprised when I heard that someone wrote a book about my home village Žerovnica. I think this is great. I think I had a happy childhood.

My family lived with my father's parents. My parents brought me and my brother to my grandparents when they went to work at six in the morning. Grandfather got up at about seven and fed the animals (cows, bulls, a horse), then grandmother got up too. She fed the pigs and chicken. We did not have cats because grandmother hated them; we had a dog. Then she started cooking lunch. Me and my brother played all the time, and when my parents came home at 2, we sometimes were still in our pajamas. Grandmother cooked lunch for all of us. We ate at about 3, after which the working day at home began for mother and father. The peasants here do not have too much land, but they work on it, so they have their own potatoes, carrots, salad, and fruits. They get milk from the cows and later meat. Nowadays, when all the people are employed [outside the village], they work at home only in the afternoons; they need machines so they can finish their work. But tractors and other equipment cost lots of money with all the oil and things that go with it. The whole policy toward farming is wrong here, ever since 1945. Then the communists and partisans took the land away from the Church, rich individuals and owners of large estates. . . . Crops were and still are badly paid, and oil wasn't cheap either. The farmers weren't motivated for their work and they didn't cultivate hills and hilly lands, just the flat and rich land. They found themselves jobs, and now there are five or six families in Žerovnica that cultivate no land at all, although they still own it. About the standard of living: an old Slovene saying says something like: he who is not satisfied with little, is not worth of bigger things. Sure, it would be terrific if we had more money, we could buy things that aren't so necessary for life. But when you think about the homeless, the starving ones around the world, and Slovenes without jobs, then we can be glad because everyone in Žerovnica has a house and a job.

There have been lots of changes lately. In Tito's time people couldn't cross the border without a visa. I still remember in the 80s, we had to pay for every border crossing, and for the next one the amount was higher, and even the number of crossings was limited. Now you can go freely wherever you want to go. This is just an example of what it was like in those days. Now that we are independent, new people are our leaders. I hope they will bring the economy out of its crisis with their new programs and ideas and assure people a better standard [of living], and therefore life in Slovenia.

Social differences existed in the past, and will be here in the future too. We tried, the socialists I mean, to create a country where all people are equal, but it did not succeed. . . .

I would love to go to the USA or to another country in the West, but only for a visit, some sightseeing and to meet some people. I wouldn't want to go somewhere where I have no one and start completely from zero. Maybe I will feel differently later in my life, I don't know.

Well, I hope this helped you a little. I wish you luck with the second book. Good bye, Andreja Godeša

Another young adult woman, Vida Mehadžič, wrote the next autobiography. Vida was born under the maiden name of Lunka in Žerovnica in 1963, and she has lived there all her life. For two years she studied at the Pedagogical Institute in nearby Postojna, and received a degree in education. This was followed by two years of sociology at the University in Ljubljana. Like Meta, she is now a teacher in the Grahovo school. Vida is a happy young woman, but knows about the hard life of the older generation and their strain of working two jobs. She reports that her family had close contacts with their Cleveland kin until her grandmother died, but that those have now ceased. Some excerpts from her autobiography, originally written in Slovene, follow:

I spent my childhood on the farm in Žerovnica, and I am still living there. . . . I am a teacher in the primary school in Grahovo. The work in the school makes me happy, and I want to do my work well. . . . I admire the beauty of our country. . . . People in Žerovnica go to their jobs in the morning, and in the afternoons they have to till their fields to produce food for their family. The village has many older inhabitants. I am living in the village that is my home and have my family there and many friends, and the landscape which I admire. I cannot work in the fields because I have plenty of work in the school. . . . Our family has relatives in Cleveland, Ohio. We wrote letters to each other, but after my grandmother and aunt died, our contacts froze. I have better contacts with my friends, professors at the University of North Carolina, with whom I correspond. . . . It would be hard for me to leave this country and to live somewhere else, as in the USA. . . . As we can see from the media or reading, life in the U.S. seems to be very materialistic, narrow-minded, artificial, and with enormous social differences. I think that in my own young country reforms will be much easier than elsewhere, although our standard of living is much lower than that in the U.S. Social differences which had been hidden before are now coming to light; they are more visible in the towns than in the villages. When the independent state of Slovenia arose, a thousand-year-old dream became a reality for the Slovene people. We are very lucky because we have gotten rid of the Serbian dictatorship in the old Yugoslavia. It was artificial to make so many nations into one country where justice was not equal for all nationalities. However, the time arrived when the world recognized Slovenia as an independent state. The world is closing its eyes to the fact that there is a war in some former republics of Yugoslavia. . . . In our country, democratic progress is only beginning, and we have much to do before the EU can receive us as an equal member in the sphere of economy, politics, and so on.

Two autobiographies follow, written in Slovene by schoolchildren on school notebook paper.

My name is Tomaž Jenc. I was born in Postojna on 12.10.1978. Our family consists of four members: my mother, my father, myself, and my younger brother. Mother is working as chief cook in a factory of transport machinery in Cerknica. Father is a machinist at the district offices in Cerknica. After they finish their jobs, they have to work on the farm. Our farm is not big, but we have plenty of work: to make fodder and feed for cows, two horses, and two pigs. I intend to go on to an electrotechnical school when I finish school. I don't know what my brother wants to do in the future. He is now in the fourth grade of the primary school. After finishing grade school, all young people from Žerovnica would like to go on to secondary school or to vocational school, rarely to the gymnasium.

Our village has 64 houses. The number of people in the village remains steady because the average family has two children. The standard of living does not allow the support of more children. We spend our free time in the summer swimming, playing football, basketball, or tennis. In the winter we spend our free time skiing and sleigh sliding. I am thinking that for now I will stay on and live in the village. The young people from Žerovnica do not like to go away from the village, but rather stay and live there. The greater part of the inhabitants work in the Brest factory.

Our family goes back many generations for about 160 years. We have relatives in Canada, but we do not have contact with them. We write letters to them only on holidays.

Our state, Slovenia, is in a difficult position now. We have not settled our border dispute with Croatia. After Slovenia's and the other republics' secession from Yugoslavia, Serbia would like to keep more territory and create terror and violence for the innocent people of Croatia and Bosnia-

Herzegovina. People had to leave their ruined homes and run away. The number of refugees in Slovenia and in the other republics is growing. The republics seceded from Yugoslavia because they wished for a better and peaceful life. Everybody wishes only to live in peace and happiness. We have to believe in better times.

Tomaž Jenc, 8th grade

The next autobiography is by another eighth-grader, Jože Telič:[8]

My name is Jožko Telič. I was born on April 25, 1978. I have a sister who is two years older than I. She will be a waitress. I hope that she will become a good waitress. My parents work in the Brest factory. My father finished secondary school and became a driver. Mother only finished grade school, and she has to work in the factory. This year I will finish grade school, and I have to decide what I want to be. In my mind, I have a vision of becoming an electrotechnician or an economist. We have a small farm. We have a milk cow, two calves, and three pigs. Mother takes care of the livestock. Of course, we help mother too. I have to work a lot on the farm, and I have no free time. By the way, I will never leave my village, Žerovnica. We have approximately seventy houses. . . . The population of Žerovnica is 250 people. In the village, the number of inhabitants is increasing. After the end of school, the young people continue to live at home. They have to have an outside job because the farms are small. They cannot live from farming alone. Young people cannot find a job after finishing school. On weekends, young people go to the discos or other entertainment. If the weather is fine, the older ones play *balina*. I love to live in the village, and would never like to exchange places with city children.

Jože Telič, 8th grade

The main themes of the autobiographies are the need for skilled or professional training for the young generation and of obtaining a job, usually away from home. But they also emphasize the strong ties that continue to bind the young to the village, which means returning home as often as possible on weekends in order to help in the fields.

Of course, the autobiographies of school children were assigned to them by their teachers and were therefore affected by the accepted norms. Yet even within these strictures the facts and attitudes revealed are of great interest.

Finally, Meta wrote her own conclusions, from which I quote here.

The people from Žerovnica don't go to church frequently, but they are again baptizing their children, now even older children whom they did not dare to baptize before. Children receive religious instruction, and they are religious. Families are smaller now than they were ten years ago. There is a low standard of living and life is very hard, and that is the reason for their small number of children. All children are born in the hospital in Postojna.[9] Another change I noticed is that sons are no longer given the name of their fathers, like Anton's son was also named Anton, etc. Now they give them different names. Another change is that in the past people from the village married within the village. But now this is no longer the case. All young people try to find jobs in the nearby factories. For now this is good, but recession is going to knock on our doors. In general, young people go to vocational school (three years) or to secondary school (four years). Besides their factory jobs they help on the farm.

I think that the relations between the sexes has changed also. In the past the source of income was the father as both peasant and factory worker. The mother took care of the children and the house. Today parents both have jobs, and they are equal. They bring up their children together. Women in the village have a greater wish to study than the men because they want to be independent from men.

Relations between neighbors are not good. I think that people are envious, and many neighbors do not speak to each other. This may be a result of the way the village is built, with the houses so close to each other. But this has not always been so. My grandmother lived in Žerovnica, and she talked to me about the relations between neighbors. At that time these relations were very good.

Now tourism is developing in this small village. I think that the villagers are very proud of their lovely country. Young people do not want to leave the village; they would like to build new houses, but this is forbidden now. They must build a few kilometers outside the village. I think this is right because the village has to retain its old architecture.

Conclusions

The system of values has been altered if not reversed since the communist years. Many objects and beliefs have changed meanings. What was once sacred, like the land and the circular field and crop rotation, has almost turned into a burden. What was once a mysterious and beautiful natural

Carnival reappears in Cerknica and Žerovnica villagers
participate

phenomenon, the Cerknica Lake, now has become a commercial attraction
for tourists. The American dream has lost its force in the modern world of
free information. The power structure in the village has been appropriated
by a new sector, the rich, young and new administrators, the former administrators who changed their affiliation to follow the times, and the most
fortunate peasant families who have been able to exploit the new economic
freedoms. The old, formerly never completely deserted since their children
aided them in the fields all year, are now left with little hope.

Indeed, the shimmering village with its striking, symmetrically divided
land strips circling the village, has become a façade disguising a world very
different from that of the early farming village. Yet, ironically, the façade
may be fated to become the most important asset of the village since,
according to the present administration's plans, the primary function of the
village is to be a tourist center. Since the 1990s peasant cultivation of the
land, partially for subsistence and partially for trade, has become an anach-
ronism. The older peasants have very little left for them. In many ways the
village is a living example of Mukařovský's self-focusing view of the aesthetic function as a preservative element and of Jakobson's artifice and
metafunction that focuses on itself and comments on the nature of the new

code. The new code is expressed in a colored brochure advertising tourism. It is adorned with a photograph of an elderly peasant driving a horse-drawn wagon covered with hay, offering a ride on a "typical peasant cart" to curious visitors who wish to experience the quaint life of the past. Is this village becoming a Skansen (an open-air museum)?

Chapter Six

The Story of the Ethnic Community in Cleveland

In chapter 1 I noted my first impressions of the well-developed and thriving ethnic Cleveland community in the 1970s in the area of St. Clair Avenue and the deterioration of the traditional community during the last decade.[1] I wish now to return to the 1880s, the beginning of Slovene immigration to Cleveland and other areas in the United States. Migrants left the home country in order to ensure the economic survival of the village that was suffering from the worldwide depression. The ethnic Slovenes, primarily of peasant stock, were used to arduous work. In spite of tremendous hardship upon the immigrants' arrival in the New World, many succeeded in climbing the economic and political ladder, or at least they helped the next generation to do so. One could ascribe their success to the tradition of work and the drive to create cooperative self-help organizations under even the most difficult circumstances.

In the letters home, the immigrants did not report the deprivations they suffered as they arrived in a new country where they had no money and no knowledge of the language. Yet immigrant literature and early migrant reminiscences reveal that many of the immigrants ceased to believe in the American dream even in the early years. In the modern era of independence, their criticisms grew and spread to the home village itself.

Immigration and Settlement History

Not only the depression years of the 1890s and 1930s affected Slovenia. The rule of primogeniture, which limited inheritance of land to one son and meant that disinherited brothers had to find another livelihood, also left its mark on the country. Thus waves of emigrants left for temporary stays that often became permanent. Earliest emigrants departed for Croatia to find temporary work in the forests. By the 1850s a few villagers had begun to sail for the United States, and this continued on an increasingly large scale until 1914 and between 1919 and 1923. Afterward immigration restrictions in the United States made entry into the country more difficult, and many Slovenes went to Germany for short work periods.

The last significant wave of Slovene immigration to the United States took place in the years 1949–56. While before World War II migrants came almost entirely for economic reasons, migrating Slovenes after the war were motivated primarily by political reasons. There were tensions between these two groups of immigrants. In this study I concentrate on those Slovenes who arrived before World War II and who shared a nostalgic sentiment for their home country.

Census data, which is not entirely reliable, list 14,332 Slovenes for Cleveland in 1910, 30,000–40,000 by the 1920s, and 46,000 by 1970. At some time during the early 1900s Cleveland became the largest Slovene settlement outside of Slovenia, although a significant number of Slovenes also settled in northeastern Ohio, Chicago-Joliet, Milwaukee–West Allis, Wisconsin, Michigan, Minnesota, and Pennsylvania. Estimates for 1980 figure the total number of Slovene immigrants and their American-born descendants in the United States between 250,000 and 350,000.

Before World War II, most Slovenes emigrated from the Slovene area of Carniola (Kranj), but also from the regions of Dolenjsko in the southeast, and Notranjsko, where Žerovnica is located, in the northwest. Typically family heads, bachelors or married men, traveled two, three, or even four times from the home village to the United States to work temporarily in the forests and coal mines in Pennsylvania, or the iron and copper mines in Michigan and Minnesota. The migrants often started out by living in dormitories and working as long hours as possible. Until the 1900s, the great majority of Slovene immigrants were young men, but after the turn of the century young women began to follow, some married and some not, joining their families. Single women typically worked for tavern owners for a period to pay off their fare advanced by the tavern owners. Young married men contemplated a fairly long or permanent stay, and when they could afford the expense, often using their meager savings or putting themselves in debt, sent for their wives and children who had been left at home. Not infrequently, after conquering early economic hardships, an enterprising

Slovene couple would invest in a large house and rent rooms to boarders, providing them with meals. Immigrants who found their way to Cleveland found work in the steel mills across from St. Clair Avenue.

Language

Slovene migrant life in the United States was characterized by a persistent attachment to the mother tongue, strengthened by Slovene cultural activities. These included Slovene language instruction in the Slovene Catholic churches or Slovene singing societies and dramatic groups using the Slovene language. The pressure to adopt English was felt at first only through contact with the authorities, but later also through contact with non-Slovene neighbors and the mass media and schools. The basic characteristic of American-Slovene linguistic culture is its bilingualism, the code switching between Slovene and English in the same speech act. In some cases the internal structure of the Slovene language has been altered under the influence of English. Thus Slovene might be incorrectly spoken under the influence of English. Not only phonology and the lexicon have been transformed, but grammatical rules have been modified. For example, Slovene Americans do not distinguish between the marked familiar and the unmarked polite form of the second person singular pronoun *ti* and *vi* and the accompanying verbal forms. Under the influence of English where the distinction is absent, they use the familiar *ti* exclusively (cf. Šabec 1995).

By the 1990s, Slovene was rarely spoken by the youth of the third and later generations. From a linguistic point of view one can generally distinguish at least three waves of immigrants. The first group to come were men, hardworking pioneers, and when wives and children joined them, all felt strong solidarity with Slovene culture and language; the second generation began to handle both American and Slovene culture, but maintained the Slovene language, feeling closely connected to the culture of the homeland. However, members of the third and later generations often felt embarrassed when their grandparents spoke Slovene. Yet one can observe some counterreaction and renewed interest in all things Slovene by the youth today, including a revival of concern for the language.

The Growth of Cooperative Societies, Cultural Institutions, Publications, the Arts, and the Parochial School

The success of the Slovene communities can be largely ascribed to the extensive cooperative activities of its members, which were organized shortly after the arrival of the first wave of immigrants. The early immigrants, lacking the economic security of supporting social institutions, developed extensive self-help institutions and cooperative associations, beginning with mutual insurance societies. Such societies did not exist in communist Slovenia, but immigrants remember the Austrian model. By the 1890s the two largest Slovene American fraternal organizations had developed: the Carniolan Slovenian Catholic Society (Kranjsko-Slovenska Katoliška Jednota [KSKJ]) formed in 1884 and later changed its name to the American Slovene Catholic Union (Ameriška Slovenska Katoliška Jednota [ASK]), and in 1904 the anticlerical Slovene National Benefit Society (Slovenska Narodna Podporna Jednota [SNPJ]) was founded. On the local level, society members were grouped into separate lodges, and the two main societies each had several lodges in Cleveland. By the mid-1970s, Slovene fraternal organizations, including the Slovene women's organization and a third insurance agency in Minnesota, had an enrollment of 185,000. Beginning in the 1920s, such organizations added to their life insurance and death benefit programs services, the promotion of educational and cultural activities, and their own newspaper and other publications. In the 1920s fraternal insurance agencies also began to form English-speaking lodges. Even before these developments, the early 1900s saw dozens of mutual aid and insurance societies, choral groups, dramatic groups, and similar organizations.

The three most important institutions in the ethnic community of the early twenties were the Catholic church, largely built by contributions of the Slovene population, the mutual insurance society, and the tavern (*gostilna*). The first Slovene national parish staffed with a Slovene priest was established in Chicago in 1891. The second, the St. Vitus (Sveti Vit) parish in Cleveland, was founded in 1893 and was also staffed by a Slovene priest. A few years later, the St. Lawrence Church (Sveti Lovrent) was established to serve the Cleveland Newburgh area, and other churches followed later. As Slovenes advanced from low-paid, unskilled labor earning perhaps $2 for a ten-hour working day, they began to develop businesses of their own, typically saloons, food stores, and restaurants. By 1910 the Slovene business community included seventy Slovene-owned ventures: clothing stores, furniture stores, funeral parlors, grocery stores specializing in Slovene food, and stores selling Slovene merchandise and Slovene language publications from Slovenia and the United States. By the second decade of the twentieth century, the size of the Slovene business community had exploded, and there were over four hundred Slovene enterprises in Cleveland.

The saloon was an important institution both economically and socially. On Saturday nights men might go from saloon to saloon. Each tavern had an accordionist who played Slovene songs on the button box. It was not hard to start a saloon since the potential owner could make an agreement with a brewery to sell only its product. Some tavern owners also assumed the role of bankers, receiving interest on their loans with an increasingly successful movement toward homeownership.

Slovene arts, music, literature, drama, song, and dance flourished in Cleveland. In 1897 the first Slovene choral society, Zora (Dawn), was formed. Later in the year it changed its name to Slovenski Sokol (Slovene Falcon) and expanded its focus to include drama and gymnastics. In 1906 the Slovene National Reading Room (Slovenska narodna čitalnica) was established. In the late twentieth century, it had its location in the Slovene National Home (Slovenski narodni dom), established in 1924 on St. Clair Avenue. The origins of the national homes can be traced to the early immigrant saloons. By 1914, there were nine national homes in Cleveland that were put to various uses. The Triglav Choral and Dramatic Society, named after the Triglav Mountain, the national symbol of Slovenia, was founded in 1913. The Sokol (Falcon) Society was established in the Collingwood suburb in 1917 and gave thirty concerts in fifteen years. The Ivan Cankar Dramatic Society organized in 1919 emerged as the most ambitious society. Its first performance was the play *The Tenth Brother* (Deseti brat), and the society produced forty-eight plays in five years. In 1924, the play *Brother Martin* (Brat Martin) was staged before 2,000 people in the National Home in Cleveland.

Other societies included Sokol (Falcon) gymnastics group, active until 1941 and a second choral society, Zvon (the Bell). By 1901 Sokol and Zvon had stopped performing, but other groups took over, the leading one being Zarja (Dawn), organized by Andrew and Josephine Turkman, the latter as its music director and conductor. Zarja has made many recordings and has repeatedly traveled to Slovenia, reintroducing old songs no longer sung in Slovenia but remembered in the villages.

In 1961, a 110-acre Slovene recreational area (*Slovenska pristava,* lit. farm building), including a large picnic area with buildings and sports facilities, was completed due to the efforts of the secular Slovene National Benefit Society, and it served as a recreational center outside of Cleveland. A second retreat, Zastava (Flag), with 75 acres, was organized by the post–World War II migrant group.

Slovene language newspapers flourished. One, *Ameriški Slovenec* (The American Slovene), first published in 1891 in Chicago and later in Cleveland, was founded by Fr. Joseph, a Slovene priest who served as a missionary among Indians of Minnesota and the Dakotas. It was published in both Slovene and two versions of English, one in standard English orthography and one in Slovene phonetic spelling. It advocated ethnic identity but also an understanding of the USA. *Ameriški Slovenec* has survived as a weekly. From 1891 to the 1990s, over one hundred Slovene language newspapers and journals had been established; but only a few lasted longer than four or five years. *Narodna beseda* (The National Word) was the first Slovene newspaper in Cleveland, appearing in 1899. There was also *Glas naroda* (The Voice of the People), founded in 1893 in New York and available in Cleveland in 1899. *Narodna beseda* changed its name to *Nova domovina* (The New Homeland), to *Amerika* in 1908, and then to *Clevelandska Amerika* (Cleveland America). It was finally renamed as *Ameriška domovina* (American Homeland) in 1914. Since the 1970s, its editor-in-chief has been Rudolph Sušelj (Susel), who has provided me with much information and general assistance.

As far as possible the ethnic Slovenes maintained a commitment to Slovene culture. Cleveland Slovene parents supported parochial schools and national parishes. The St. Vitus and St. Lawrence parishes each had their own parochial schools and could not accept all that applied. In 1910, St. Vitus had 450 students and only six teachers, thus leading to the establishment of a new school. By 1930, English had become the language of instruction, with Slovene relegated to special afternoon classes.

By the early twentieth century the Slovene community had become a developed society. With a second generation appearing in the first decade of the twentieth century, the community diversified, and many more organizations were formed. By 1914 *Clevelandska Amerika* listed fifty-three Cleveland area lodges affiliated with various national organizations and a total membership of 7,500. By then there were twenty independent insurance agencies and nine educational, artistic, or economic societies, adding another 3,000 members.

The early Slovene community retained close relations with kin back home. Since 1950, thousands of immigrants and American Slovenes have visited Slovenia, and villagers from the homeland have frequently come to Cleveland. I have noted that the most important internal variation within the ethnic community derived from the split between the politically motivated immigrants and the economically motivated peasants. However, there were also religious variations since many individuals did not practice Catholicism, some of them even holding strongly anticlerical attitudes following Old World socialist traditions. Two parallel sets of economic and cultural organizations reflected the rift between the religious and the secular groups, but this apparently has not decreased the strong sense of ethnic identity within either.

The Inner Story of the Migrants' Early Experiences

Until now our story of the Slovene ethnic community has been a linear historical account of bare facts, which does not disclose subjective points of view of the migrants who came to the shores of the United States.

But what of their illusions and disillusions, their ways of coping? To elucidate the inner story, I record reflections of settlers young and old who describe their early experiences in the United States. I also draw on some written narratives such as novels, autobiographies, biographies, chronicles, and travel accounts by Slovene Americans. Vast areas of anthropological information relating to this ethnic culture do not emerge from purely factual and referential sources such as encyclopedias or histories. Yet a reader may glean much from an interpretation of the aesthetic, emotive, and frequently ambiguous elements in personal narrations.

In their recollections of life in peasant villages in Slovenia, Slovene Americans recall a traditional lifestyle existing before World War II. In their preservation of Slovene culture in the New World they have further retained traditional ways that often disappeared decades ago in the home villages. In addition, the overseas ethnic communities have often transformed the meaning of traditional ways or objects.

I contrast here two intersecting themes, that of poverty and that of music, particularly in its expression in song. The perspective of traditional poverty is opposed to the New World view that poverty is something one must believe one can overcome, and as migrants succeeded in realizing this goal, they began to share the idealistic American outlook, mitigated by their nostalgic recollections of the village past. The second theme, Slovene music and song, powerfully evokes the village aura, all the more poignantly for those who knew the character of the village during the communist rule since much of this music was silenced during those years.

I turn now to two life histories rendered in the first person (my own comments added in brackets), in which the two related themes interact.

Marija, whose parents come from Slovene villages, was born in 1915 in Pennsylvania and moved to Cleveland as a young woman. She has since lived in the traditional Slovene section of Cleveland's inner city. The following is her story:

POVERTY

My father went to West Virginia as a lumberjack. But in 1908 he wanted to go home. He went back to his village, but he had to return again to the United States. In West Virginia he met my mother, a Slovene woman who came with a group of girls. They established a boarding house and took in sixty boarders, and I and my friends worked as a group in shifts. We baked bread outdoors like in the old days and only slept four hours, but the men got fresh bread every day. My father and mother married and stayed in West Virginia until 1920. It was a rough life. The guys stayed in the woods the whole week. They came into town to drink, dance, play cards and then went back again to the forest. Women were slaves. When I was five years old and it was time for children to return to school, my mother and father returned to my father's village. We were ten children. My father was spoiled by the USA, so he spent all the money in taverns. He came back to his village with lots of money, but he drank it all up. My mother did all the work. I was always sick as a child, and there was no money. My mother took a basket of potatoes to the doctor to pay him for examining me. We had an average-sized farm and were very poor. Ninety percent of the people in the village lived like that. Life in the village was hard work. At twelve years no one had ever bought me a dress.

You had to break a hole through the ice to wash clothes until your fingers were frostbitten. I went to America when I was twenty-two. My mother cried when I left and said she hoped I would have a better life in America. I went to Johnston, Pennsylvania where my aunt was living. It was just after the depression. In 1937 I went to Cleveland and worked in a tavern as a waitress at $8 a week, seven days a week, twelve to fourteen hours a day and Friday to midnight. I went to night school and learned English. When you come from Europe you're full of energy and load hay like any guy. I had to work like a man.

I quit working in the tavern when my child was born; then I worked for fourteen years in a factory when my child went to school. The factory made parts for rifles. I became an inspector. My husband also worked in the factory. We bought a two-family house and rented out one side. Then I gave up the factory and became a part-time cook for weddings.

I have returned to Slovenia four times since the war. But earlier I did not write. I was ashamed to admit it, but I did not have enough money to help my people earlier. To Slovenes, America is a heaven, but for me this was not the case. I was too proud to admit that I was not doing well. So I was silent. I wrote no letters. I did not buy anything until the house was paid off. I am not like young people who spend on anything.

MUSIC

I loved to sing and dance when I was a child living in my village. Sunday afternoons and Saturday evenings, these were the most beautiful part of growing up. I knew five hundred songs. Everyone joined in singing. I played in operettas and sang all the time. At weddings we had an accordion player. The wedding took three days. When I looked for a job in Cleveland, I also looked for group where I could sing. I was a good singer. I found a singing group in 1937. I needed the company. And I returned to Slovenia three times with the Cleveland Slovene choral society Zarja. During the last war I worked for Slovenia as did all Slovenes abroad. I worked for the Red Cross and we gave concerts for the benefit of Yugoslavia.

I speak Slovene all the time and my daughter speaks it beautifully. I feel strongly about singing. We sing all the time because we want to and not for profit. They must know about our songs in Slovenia. They are forgetting their past. When we went back we took operas to Slovenia.

I turn now to the life story of another second-generation Slovene migrant, Janez, who was born in Pennsylvania. His parents had emigrated to the United States from Slovene villages. Our discussions took place on Janez's front porch in Cleveland. His comments were broken by his intermittent singing. He was a member of Zarja. His wife served us iced tea and commented that her husband tells good stories and loves to talk. Both the exterior and interior of the house are profuse with signs of the ethnic culture. There is a vegetable garden bordered by flowers, and the linden tree. There is also a wooden bench in front of the house, just as one finds in Slovene villages. Inside the house there are two objects that our informant discusses during his life history. I interpret both as condensed polysemic signs. One object was a lump of coal placed noticeably on a desk to show, as Janez said, that he and his father had been miners. He told us that he promised his father that the piece of coal would always remain in its place. It indexically signifies the hard work and poverty in the New World, which ultimately led to the relatively comfortable house and furnishings they now possessed.

The second object was a small-scale model of a *kozolec,* the traditional Slovene rack for drying hay. Janez remarked that he had made a full-scale *kozolec* on his land. He planned to extend the roof of the *kozolec* to form an overhang just as in Slovenia. He wanted to make a place for a pitchfork and room for a wagon to pull in. The *kozolec* would be standing on the "farm" of the Slovene Mutual Benefit Society outside of Cleveland. The "farm" of the other wing of migrants already had a large concrete *kozolec* marking its entrance. Again, context determined the montage-like iconic, indexical, and symbolic character of this structure turned aesthetic (rather than practical).

POVERTY

My father had come to the United States in 1905 at the age of eighteen. But when I was five years old, we went back to my father's village in Slovenia. There were six children. My mother's family were *bajtars* [peasants with little or no land]. They had one cow, one pig and were too poor for even a dog or cat. But they had a *kozolec*. My father also was a *bajtar*. He had only one or two cows, two pigs, and some chickens so that he could have eggs to bring to the store to exchange for oil and sugar. We had no horse. We had to carry wheat on our backs down into the valley to be milled. There were flowers in every window. They might not have time to whitewash every house. Oh, beautiful Slovenia!

The *kozolec,* the traditional hayrack that dots villagers' fields in Slovenia

MUSIC

My father did not want to go to the United States and leave his singing group's church choir. In the evenings he wandered around the village and sang. They had started having mixed choruses in the church. The *župnik* [parish priest] promoted singing. But he objected to some songs as too peppy. I was an altar boy, I loved to sing. Everyone in Slovenia knew songs. I learned them from my mother.

My father said he was going to save up some money, so in 1932 he went back to Pennsylvania and worked in the mines. The Slovenes there were good and generous, and he got lodging and food. We followed him, and in 1936 I also got a job in the mines. It was 384 feet down. My father spent all his life in the mines, and I went with him. I was his buddy. When I was a coal miner, I loaded nine tons a day. Now this is all mechanized. The ceiling was quite high, and I did not have to crawl. But I never could get used to mining.

Music and Economic Success in Cleveland

Another immigrant related the following story:

> One day in 1941 in Pennsylvania, my brother and I heard Slovene songs from a
> singing group from Cleveland. We got so homesick for these songs. We were
> thirsty for this stuff. It was the day of the solidarity parade in Pennsylvania
> and my father was going to the parade. My twin brother and I picked up and
> went to Cleveland. For three weeks we worked in the foundry. But it was too
> hot. It was at 42nd Street and St. Clair Avenue. I met the members of Zarja
> when I went to the Slovene Home. The boys were singing in the clubroom. My
> brother and I joined. We didn't lose any time. In 1949 I got a job in a trucking
> firm and I am still there, after twenty-five years. But it will close its doors next
> year. It was a pleasant place to work. Good union, good fringe benefits. Now it
> is day-to-day. For us guys eligible for pension it's not bad, but it's not good for
> the ones who have only been here twenty years and no pension.
>
> All these years I sang with Zarja. It's fortunate that they can stand me. That
> was my only tranquilizer. I never need more than aspirin. But in Pennsylvania
> we never learned so much that we could put a concert on. I love to sing and to
> act in plays. We had plays in the Collingwood Workmen's Home. I used to
> belong to the Ivan Cankar Dramatic Club. But it is no more. Today we do not
> have a good director and people can't read and memorize Slovene. Last night
> we had a singing rehearsal. It was wonderful. It makes me feel good.
>
> I was fortunate, I was born not too soon and not too late. My father
> worked so hard in the mines. When I came to Cleveland, the Slovene Home
> was already there and we were ready to sing and act in plays there.
>
> There is no bunch like Zarja. So funny, so cooperative and so kind. I'm
> going to put in a cement foundation for the *kozolec* on the SNPJ farm. Too
> bad my parents are not alive. They would get a kick out of the *kozolec*. It is
> just like the one near my mother's house.

Written Documents

For my last example I look at some selections from written documents by
Slovene Americans, one by a Slovene woman of the first generation of
immigrants, Mary Molek, and two by her husband, Ivan Molek, a Slovene
immigrant who was born in Slovenia.

Mary Molek wrote *Immigrant Woman* in 1976. This text (written in

English) takes the form of a memoir, the story of Mary Molek's mother, but also of herself and her husband. *Two Worlds* was written by Ivan Molek in Slovene in 1932, Mary Molek translated it into English, in which language it appeared in 1978. This novel tells the story of the migrant Anton, and has strong autobiographical components. The English version of *Slovene Immigrant History, 1900–1950: Autobiographical Sketches,* authored by Ivan Molek and translated by Mary Molek from the Slovene manuscript entitled *Over Hill and Dale,* was published in 1979.

These narratives, which are first of all self-referential, juxtapose the two cultural traditions in ethnic culture, the traditional culture and the host culture. As Peirce wrote, there is a double consciousness in all perception, a consciousness of an ego and a consciousness of a non-ego, acting directly upon each other (CP 5.45). But they simply form the basis for more complex referrals to outside reality and to other voices. As Bakhtin wrote, there is double voicing: The informant provides the authorial voice, readers or listeners project their own interpretation, a second voice, and interpreters inject a third voice into the polysemic tale. And thinking of this many-leveled quality and its codes, I consider the reflexivity of the narratives, the issues of identity, and also the implicit metacommentary on the nature of Slovene ethnic culture as Mary tells her mother's story.

A patchwork quilt, a collage, bits, snatches, and parts. These are the terms Mary Molek chooses to characterize the life structure of the immigrant woman, her mother, as seen through the eyes of her oldest child, the author herself. Who is the heroine of this tale? Mary, "the oldest," born in a mining town in Kansas in 1909, or the mother who arrived in the New World as a young woman and who lived to the age of 85, never to return to her homeland?

If existence lies in opposition, in twoness (cf. Jakobson's discussion of Peirce 1977, 1029), then it emerges well from the ethnic experience that, as Mary writes, is a pastiche of dichotomies—interwoven, interpenetrating, conflicting. The "oldest" herself becomes an urban, educated, professional intellectual woman, a psychologist who married, and becomes partner to, an urban revolutionary writer and thinker. The "oldest," that is how the daughter refers to herself, is the reverse of the mother whose every value represents antithetical positions to those of her daughter. And yet deeper meanings underlie and unite oppositions, since ethnic experience is a powerful tie between the Americanized daughter and the mother who adheres to Slovene traditional values. Stubborn, uncompromising values, pride, drive, inventiveness, and ingenuity are traits that forever unite these polar individuals.

Mary, the author, was born unattended in 1909, in a small shack, a company house provided by the owners of the local mine. Her mother had chosen America to have a better chance at aiding her elderly village parents. She believed that she would return home in two years. She came at the behest of the young man she was to marry, an earlier immigrant, the Slovene man who had left the village alone to work in the mines and await the arrival of the woman for whom he had sent. Her mother's words, quoted by her daughter, send a sad message. "If I had known, I never would have come." For instead of returning home in two years, instead of arriving in a land of plenty, and instead of marrying a successful pioneer, she married an indebted and exploited miner, and, as a seamstress and worker of all tasks, labored to free the family from the accumulated debts for steamship tickets, bridal clothes, wedding ceremonies. The pattern continued for years. Indebtedness contradicted village norms, so already the mother was put into conflict. She coped by never discarding anything. Dandelions and homemade bread were common meals. No one ever saw a doctor. No one was ever idle. The few trees in the barren landscape near the small house were guarded and more were planted. The family communicated in an amalgam of English and Slovene that others understood fairly well. No one ever consciously borrowed. The "oldest" was reared to help her mother escape from the debt no amount of work could prevent.

The child, the "oldest," is raised in fear of transgression. She has to return the 25 cents given to her when she delivers a dress. She has to give up the few pennies saved over months to the threatening priest collecting local dues. She works in the local saloon but never crosses any boundary or speaks to the clientele.

While bootlegging meant profits for many during Prohibition, the local mines, church, company store, parochial schools, and saloon owners presented a total, inescapable structure for the mother. Men at least could visit the saloon; people like "the oldest" could find liberation in education. Yet the mother was shackled.

After the death of Mary's father, urged by her well-meaning children, the mother gave up her frame house, the rose bushes, the small garden, the intermittent animals, some chickens, a cow, a cat to move to an urban apartment. Here, the meaning of life finally disappeared, as it had already begun to do several times before: upon arrival in Kansas; on the day of the "oldest's" wedding to a stranger from the city; on the day the letter from the village said that her own mother had died, that her father would take over the little place until he could locate a younger brother, and that all would be better "when you come back"; on the day the barn burned down without insurance; on the day the "oldest" moved to the nearby town to teach school.

The tribute to the immigrant woman by the "oldest" leaves a question. What makes the ethnic collage? The daughter who brings to life and makes palpable, in novels and in biography, traditions that do not die, and who, as a scientist, pioneers ethnic archives at universities? Or the mother who became a hardworking *bricoleur* in the new society and supported her child's struggle to attain a profession? Indeed, they are both ethnic collages.

I trace the opposition between Mary Molek, the child of an immigrant, and her mother, a true immigrant. The author claims to document the American experience as seen through her mother's eyes. Thus we obtain a double view in which the ethnic world of the daughter is juxtaposed to the view that the daughter ascribes to her mother. This work presents, then, two counterposed individuals. There is first of all the mother who, like Lotman's hero in a plot text, is to some extent a hero since she crosses the boundaries from home to the New World. However, she is equipped only with Old World weapons in her struggle for a livelihood in the New World. In this sense she may be inventive but limited. Yet her very existence and actions in the New World milieu suggest an explicit montage. She is contrasted to her daughter who becomes a hero in crossing boundaries from the ethnic culture outward into the host culture and, with the advantage of the support from her mother, succeeds in becoming a trained scientist. And it is this new ability that enables her to then take a double view, to document her own ethnic heritage.

Poverty and the loss of closeness in the peasant family inscribe the mother's fate. "Krazzy Fools" the mother calls all those who participate in commercial American culture symbolized by radio, television, or modern kitchen equipment. The mother also rejects such intellectual activities as learning or reading, all of which she sees as threatening, an attitude that reveals a well-known traditional but changing value in the peasant village, namely that anything that appears to introduce new worlds to the peasant family and to rob them of their children should be looked upon with suspicion. The explicit montage, in Lotman's sense, of the peasant mother counterposed to the new environment is placed against the implicit montages of the various stages of the daughter's personality as she escapes to an educated life and recreates the immigrant culture in her writings.

In *Two Worlds* by Ivan Molek, I trace a double opposition that is what I call the ethnic network map, alloyed to human relations of a special kind, as opposed to the official geographic maps of the United States, which do not express human relationships. An immigrant, the peasant Anton (a disguised Ivan, referred to here by his true name Ivan), leaves his Slovene village and finds disillusionment in the United States. I see him as another Lotmanian boundary-crossing hero. Rejecting the drudgery and smallness of the peasant village while still expressing strong emotional ties to it, the adventurer leaves for the "land of plenty," thinking, as Mary Molek's mother had done, that he would depart only for a few years in order to help the ones at home.

Ivan's arrival in the United States is followed by a trek across the country to the factories and steel towns of middle America. Penniless and barely knowing a word of English, Ivan looks in each new town for a Slovene friend or an old neighbor from home. This meant searching for a Slovene boardinghouse near a factory, a Slovene saloon, or a Slovene church. These structures function as surrogates for home. They shelter the migrant while Slovene friends help find him work. Ivan always sends home part of the meager pay to support the family that remained behind.

The folk theme of the wandering hero overcoming obstacles appears in greater detail in Ivan Molek's work entitled *Slovene Immigrant History, 1900–1950: Autobiographical Sketches,* which relates Ivan's own story of leaving his Slovene village in the Bela Krajina near the Hungarian border. The narrative tells that Ivan's wanderings convey his disillusionment. Even his realization, at last, of an intellectual and literary life does not succeed entirely because factions and severe competition in the ethnic cultural and political world bring about his defeat when he attempts to remain uncompromising in relation to his ideals.

A network map of the United States emerges. Here, not the rivers, mountains, and towns, serve as markers, but rather migrants and their relatives and friends who dot the landscape with their havens that rescue the wanderer. This network opposes the official map of the lonely landscape, the desolate urban sites, the strange faces and foreign language, the road maps and train schedules, and official boundaries. Thus for the Slovene wanderer, boundaries are determined by the area occupied by members of the ethnic culture as opposed to those of non-Slovenes. Generally, migrants only crossed these boundaries to get to the next and closest subsection of this ethnic culture. Thus the opposition we/other is marked by the boundaries of space occupied by Slovene immigrants in contrast to those nameless peoples' space outlined by official maps. Informal contacts and letters written to the potential migrant spread the knowledge of the ethnic boundaries.

To take one example from the narrative: in 1900, upon Ivan's arrival in the United States, he goes to Steeltown, Pennsylvania, the first stop after the train leaves New York. He alights and does not see the familiar face he expected to find; his friend Zavrshnik is not at the station. "I carefully observed the people. Since I had heard Steeltown was full of Slovenes, I was bound to meet one. . . . Then I had a sudden awareness that my cane was superfluous. I had met hundreds of men and not one with a cane." Abandoning his cane he goes back to the station. "Someone was calling to me. 'Hey, Molek.' It was Jozhe Stariha—a neighbor from Hrib who came to America last year" (2).

At least subliminally it seems that Ivan was aware of the sign quality of the cane and its different meanings at home and in America. While at home it marked the dignity of the peasant male, in the new environment it was transformed into an embarrassing item. Here for Ivan it only marked its owner as "different" and thus subject to ridicule. The sign quality of the cane has many levels. Thus as Ivan rejects the cane, he does not realize that in the New World a cane either adorns a gentleman of high status or aids someone who needs it for physical reasons.

As Ivan Molek continues to walk with his friend, he comes to a large frame building occupied by ten families, including boarders. "To enter this house was to come into a new Metlika," Ivan writes. "I soon met all my schoolmates and acquaintances of my youth." A welcoming beer-drinking celebration that lasted all afternoon begins, evoking traditional village hospitality (22–24). After a few days, the lodging master, who organized Slovene music in the area, introduces Ivan to the foreman of the factory, and he gets his first job.

Typically, as work diminishes in one area, Ivan hops a freight train, and the same story is repeated. Travels to other towns to get better jobs are described. Ivan writes about arriving in Reading, Pennsylvania, "I also found Slovenes and a house full of Slovene boarders, all from the Metlika vicinity. They staged the usual welcome with a keg of beer" (49).

Later Ivan arrives in Calumet, Michigan, one of the oldest Slovene settlements in the United States (the oldest being Brockway, Minnesota, which was settled in 1865). When Ivan alights from the train, "I walked towards the city and looked at the signs in the store window. On the first building across the street I read: Mihael Schmalzel, Slovenian tavern," and he notes Slovene shops and saloons everywhere. He writes: "I felt at home" (56).

The immigrant experience, extrapolated from the writings of Ivan and Mary Molek, is characterized by complex ties to the homeland and strong obligations between kin and friends. The following types of comments suggest the latter: Ivan wrote that his mother's letters written for her by her sister (since his mother was illiterate) showed irritation and reproach since not enough remittances arrived. Of course his mother could not know of all his endeavors and difficulties, for he never told her of the hardships that he had to undergo to send money home. Recalling the close relations at home, Ivan writes that "in my village, all adults were called Uncle and Aunt. I grew up more under the influence of my uncles than my parents" (11). When Ivan's father died, for example, the neighbors in the village maintained close relationships, giving the boy a feeling of at-homeness. A second home, almost closer than his first, was that of his grandparents, where the parents left Ivan when they hired out to work in other fields.

Mary Molek concludes her work *Immigrant Woman* with a telling quotation from Ibsen, "His native place is to a man's foot what the root is to a tree. If need for his work lies not there, his deeds were doomed and his tale is told" (65).

Conclusion

I am arguing that the immigrant experiences of the Slovenes that we are describing can be interpreted as metaphorical transformations of the home villages to an alien environment, and that this transformation is communicated through the most diverse verbal and nonverbal signs, particularly through montage confrontations creating complex texts that point to new similarities and/or differences.

All these narratives, oral and written, bear an indirect relation to the broader cultural context, and thus they give us anthropological information about the ethnic culture in various ways. The meanings of these works, as they are interpreted by an outsider, a detached person with some knowledge of the traditional culture, not only provide referential data but also convey, through various tropes and aesthetic components, the subjective imagination and point of view of the Slovene migrant.

IV

Semiotic Portraits

Chapter Seven

Semiotic Portraits in Cultural Context

Changes in the Larger Society and Their Psychological Consequences

The final chapter takes up the challenge of semiotic portraits. I preface it by a brief review of the most recent changes in the two communities and an assessment of the problem that has haunted this study, that is, how, in the search for meaning, the ethnographer grapples with the ambiguity and dynamism of ethnic groups. Then follows an exploration of dialogic relations in three cases that I consider extended human signs. Each case reaches back and forth between the two communities, the villagers at home and their ethnic relatives in Cleveland and Hibbing. And each is engulfed in major changes, economic and social, having significant cultural and psychological consequences. As these examples demonstrate, changes in the hierarchy of social levels and in the power structure cannot be separated from global modernism and postmodern issues. Most markedly, the three-generation household has been fast disappearing.

In the village the changing economy and modernization have most heavily and negatively influenced the older villagers, while they have had positive effects on the youth, even if they cause them some psychological conflict. In the ethnic community in the United States, the expanding economy has had some positive effects on the situation of the elders, even if they remain nostalgic about the past, while the youth have profited most by modernization. Both situations affect the ego strength and psychology of these individuals as they cope with changes that are dramatic if not revolutionary (as in the case of the village).

In both cases the architecture of houses functions as an outward clue to inner change. In Cleveland, the abandonment of the traditional houses in the St. Clair area, so reminiscent of village structures, for ranch-style houses in the suburbs was accompanied by the erection of modern institutions for the elders. While the official policy in Žerovnica attempted to preserve the architectural and spatial structure of the village as a bare artifice, in Cleveland there were no efforts to prevent the deterioration of the once vibrant ethnic community dotted with shops, restaurants, and bookstores on St. Clair Avenue.

The shifts affect the older generations in contrasting ways, since elders are not protected as the modern world impinges on the village, but they are well provided for by the Americanized ethnic community. On the other hand, affinities exist between the village youth and those growing up in the ethnic community: both groups benefit from education for skilled or professional employment. Thus from changing architecture to forces emanating from outside, all concomitant with modernization, the structure of the family has changed in both communities.

To explore the inner consequences of the road to modernization, I cite the psychiatrist-anthropologist Arthur Kleinman, who deplores the neglect by psychiatrists and anthropologists of the interrelation between cultural forces and psychological states of being (1988, xi). His and other cross-cultural findings, Kleinman warns, involve "situations of uprooting, refugee status, and forced acculturation [that are] often associated with psychiatric disorders" (2). Furthermore, Kleinman notes that some cultures appear to inculcate their members against particular disorders (3).

I ask how these generalizations apply to our two communities. Slovene in-group feeling, social solidarity, and work ethic has accounted for considerable ego strength of the villagers throughout their history, enabling them to weather feudalism, and the trials of war and emigration. But under communism a general depression, apathy, and fatalism emerged as initiative and self-reliance were lost to the government (although there remained a strong will to fight and to find ways to get around official restraints). Similarly, the threatening, early immigrant experience tested the courage and fortitude of the migrants, but their own cultural traditions generally served them well.

The contrasting fate of the aged demonstrates the importance of contextual issues that Kleinman stresses. Thus modernization broke down one of the strongest norms in the village, namely the prestige of, and respect for, the elders who today seem lost and despondent. The drive for economic gain overwhelmed the youth, and they had to live elsewhere. Furthermore, while villagers never found themselves in the position of refugees, they were for centuries subject to the rule of other nations. And throughout the communist decades they felt threatened since they continually feared the confiscation of their agricultural lands or forests lands. Poverty was prevalent, economic structures and bureaucratic centralism hedged them in, and they were without retirement pensions or with an inadequate one, and only limited health insurance. Kleinman notes that an anthropological sensibility must be aware of cultural assumptions and also of "irony, paradox, ambiguity, drama, tragedy, humor . . . [which] are the elemental conditions of the humanities" (17).

Ironically, independent Slovenia has no solution for the plight of the older peasants, since the strong and able younger generation are joining the commercial world of tourism or technological training and forsaking the dwindling farming economy. The old have lost their *esprit,* they are tired and overworked, and the new plans of the *občina* seem to offer no room for them.

In Cleveland, on the other hand, support of the aged underwent a transformation. By 1976, the Slovene community had erected at least two institutions for the elderly, an assisted living community and a nursing home. Here ethnic solidarity has survived and undergone fortification. I gave a lecture at the assisted living facility about my work, and I believe almost all the residents attended. The audience was extremely interested in what I had to say about village life in Slovenia, and they made a very positive impression, alert, well-dressed, and dignified. The facility and its surroundings were very attractive.

The ethnic community also established its own nursing home. When I visited it in the 1970s, I found it well-kept and clean. A friendly mood and rapport pervaded among the patients and the personnel, which contrasted with the often commercial, impersonal, and dreary atmosphere in many American nursing homes. There was a lively give-and-take among the patients, some of whom were in wheelchairs. I saw none sitting isolated and alone.

Theoretical Issues Pertaining to Fieldwork:
The Authoritative Voice, Ethnicity, and Nostalgia

I turn once more to the issue of the ethnographer's own semiotic world and how it is to be accounted for and brought into consciousness. We must inhibit the ethnographer's authoritative voice and point of view as far as possible, but not entirely, not only because this would be impossible, but also because any analysis must have a general theoretical background that organizes the ethnographer's perceptions.

The complexities of accounting for the authoritative voice of the ethnographer, whose cultural background may or may not be similar to the group being studied, shades into the overworked term "ethnicity." The Hungarian anthropologist Tamás Hofer emphasized the "impact of the more or less similar 'ethnic' or 'national' cultural baggage in the case of ethnographers coming from the same national society" (1996, 89). Hofer concerns himself primarily with a European dilemma, that of Europeans of differing ethnic backgrounds studying other Europeans or of nationals investigating sectors of their own population. My own fieldwork is a composite of these problems: in Slovenia, I as an American with a Czech-born and reared American husband, was looking at a very different ethnic culture than my own. But in Cleveland, as Americans, we were looking at ethnic Slovene Americans. The American outlook toward ethnic groups has changed over time. Traditionally, American ethnologists studying American ethnic groups projected the melting pot ideal, but the reality of pluralism and multiculturalism, not normatively viewed as a sign of discord, has superseded that perspective. But even in the United States, the country that gave birth to the concept of the right to ethnic self-determination, this positive view is threatened by dissension.

Americans share with Slovene villagers and ethnic Slovenes the lack of a historical traditional elite, the Slovene elite having been replaced by the Germans under the Austro-Hungarian monarchy. Nor did a genuine peasantry in the European sense (emerging from feudalism) ever emerge in America. Yet America is built of ethnic groups that bring with them their own traditions, which create the kind of transnationalism at issue in this study. In the case of the Slovene Americans, the values embedded in their folk culture account for the strong sense of loyalty to family, village, and nation, and for the formation of cooperative organizations similar to those established in the home country under the Hapsburg monarchy. Strong, homogeneous Slovene cultural values have not disappeared under the influence of American individualism and cutthroat competition.

The whole area of ethnicity is complex, and we lack a single definition for this dynamic domain that refers to widely differing phenomena having in common little more than self-identity and a feeling of belonging to one culture as opposed to another. However complex and conscious these various feelings, their emotive and aesthetic components depend on many variables, not the least of which are cultural context, memories of historical events, and experience in general. As Peirce has written, "experience is our only teacher." A quick review of theories highlighting the values of intertextualities and their subtle interrelationships will serve us well here. As mentioned earlier, Bogatyrev was one of the first to consider costumes as signs, the most general one, which I call a metasign, overriding all others: "our culture," not theirs. Bakhtin's works, such as *Rabelais and His World,* might be posited as a symphonic play on ethnic identity and its dynamic reversals.

Lotman and Uspensky both implied ethnic identity throughout their work, for example in the treatment of Russians who adopted and even internalized other identities, or of Tolstoy who masqueraded as a peasant as he wandered across the landscape.

Barthes held that "intertextuality cannot be reduced to the question of literary influences. It comprises the whole field of contemporary and historical languages as reflected within the text" (1975, 995, as discussed in Noth 1990, 975).

Human Signs in Cultural Context

I see the dramatis personae, the actors in the stories I discuss who cross boundaries, as heroes in plot texts. The foundation of explicit montage, that is the juxtaposition of elements from different semantic domains, is in this case exemplified by villagers or ethnic Slovenes in whose ethos two worldviews partake. If they are villagers who have not emigrated, their worldview combines that of the village world with the imagined one of Cleveland.

When villagers secretly sell piglets in private or smuggle horses and butter to Italy, we are dealing with implicit montage because existing elements have simply undergone reorganization.

Certainly explicit and implicit montage, which I see as versions of both metonymic metaphors and of linear and circular plot and narration, overlap and interpenetrate. Performances and mentalities of individuals cannot simply and exclusively be classed as having particular attributes. For purposes of analysis, devices such as these can help the outsider understand the inner world of these people. Yet I do not wish to imply that the actors themselves necessarily see themselves as taking part in such symbolic meanings. Additionally, it is helpful for the observer to abstract from the text an artistic element since such texts play with the unexpected, pulling together changing moods or forms, or juxtaposing antithetical elements that highlight new similarities. Furthermore, I see a family resemblance between the ethnic actor and the actor in a theater, both of whom are able to become transfigured, as Bogatyrev wrote, moving from one world to another.

I quote Pelc here as an introduction to those I shall describe:

> The narrator may narrate about . . . himself. If this takes place, . . . he appears in a double role: as a narrating subject and as an object of the narrative. . . . A person who is painting his self-portrait is both the painter and the model. The semantic relation accordingly holds between the signs that form the narrative and the narrator as their extralinguistic referent. It remains a semantic relation if the narrative pertains to the narrator's mental experience. (Pelc 1971, 12–13)

In the spirit of Pelc's remarks, the narrator may be a double, thus reflexive, sign, and also a sign of a nonreflexive narration about the context, including the history of an epoch. Thus the history of the life of a community can also serve as a sign.

The following materials are interpretations that I have labeled as extended human signs not bounded by a single individual or place. In this sense, I see an extended human sign as the interweaving of highly flexible groups of individuals, united not only by kinship but by common loyalties to particular places, and also by a feeling of double identity, both Slovene and American, real or imagined.

The Extended Human Sign of Matija Rok, His Family in Slovenia,
and His Relatives in Hibbing

Earlier in this study, I considered the issues of space-time and boundaries as
perceived in transnational consciousness as relativized to the actors' perceptions. Here I consider a three-generation extended human sign: my principal informant during my stays in the village during 1960s and early 1970s,
Matija Rok and his wife Marija constitute the first generation, his daughter
Marija and his son-in-law Anton (Tone) Primožič the second, and Marija
and Tone's daughters the third. All lived in the same house. I also include in
this extended human sign Matija Rok's sister and her husband, both from
Žerovnica, who live as ethnic Slovenes in Hibbing, Minnesota. The semi-
otization of certain practical objects also takes part in the transnational
drama.

The late Matija Rok, the *podžupan* (headman) of the village for many
years, was an excellent raconteur. He had guarded village records from
earliest times, tracing land holdings and their distribution, changes in practices such as the abolition of the common grazing land (*gmajna*), and the
awarding of some forest land to the peasants. He always wore a fedora hat
inside and out, the sign in the village of the head of the household (*gospodar*). When Anton Primožič became the *gospodar* after his father-in-law's
death, he followed the same custom. Since the Roks had only one daughter
and no son, Anton, the daughter's husband, moved into her house. Matija
and his wife Marija, as well as their daughter Marija and her husband
Anton, and also Marija's and Anton's two daughters, Marija and Tončka
(Antonia) when old enough, worked in the fields prodigiously, and the men
also lumbered. The family's holdings were average size (one quarter *zemlja*)
and, like most families, they sent one member, Anton, to the nearby furniture factory Brest for economic survival. Workdays, including at least partial Sundays, were long. The Rok family house, as all the others in this
village, was so close to the neighboring ones that there was barely space to
walk between them. While I spent long hours with the Rok family, I never
observed any communication with the neighboring house, which I believe
is not uncommon. The Rok house, like all the village houses, was fronted by
a garden, flowers, a bench, and a fence, all enclosing a small space. The

kitchen was the central room for conversation, and I sat, frequently with my husband, around the kitchen table with Matija as he searched his records and maps. His wife served us Turkish coffee, *slivovka* (plum brandy), sausage, bread, and sweets, no matter what time of day we came. Matija's wife and daughter stood much of the time while Matija, Anton, my husband, and I sat around the small kitchen table. However, Marija Rok frequently joined in the conversation. The entire family was extremely hospitable and showed great interest in our work, which we described as a historical study of the village for American students of ethnology. Tone often had to leave for agricultural chores or was at work in the factory, to which he commuted by moped. Since villagers felt that no one was interested in them, and in fact peasants were looked upon as the lowest stratum of society, almost all villagers welcomed the visiting foreigners who broke up the daily tedium, valued them, and wished to write about them.

It is easy to view Matija Rok as a sign of his village culture given his peasant workclothes and boots, the hat symbolizing authority, and his typical behavior marked by dry humor. He combined within him the most prized village values, independence, industriousness, frugality, and pride, and stood as a repository of all that was known of the village past. Matija's moods changed from humor to serious reflection or controlled anger and resignation when he described the communist restrictions, the low value put on the peasant, and the loss of much village autonomy. He also expressed apprehension that nearby Marof might confiscate cultivable land or forests, and he spoke contemptuously of the party bureaucrats of urban origin who inefficiently ran the cooperative farm bordering on village land. His long tales of the village's history, often supported by documents, marked him as a scholar and a narrator. He was a culture hero in Lotman's sense, not bound by official and bureaucratic rules and boundaries and remaining a free thinker who, as a former headman, had designed a new role for himself, that of the unofficial village historian. Is not Matija's narration an example of Bakhtin's heteroglossia? For much of his story had an ironic edge, the proud history of the village in the context of its decline under the communist regime.

Tone emulated Matija in every way and shared his point of view; indeed, he had a similar personality. Tone and Marija's two daughters, Marija and Tončka, whom we knew as infants, children, and teenagers, and as young

Matija Rok and his son-in-law Anton Primožič logging. The
villagers looked upon the forest as their gold reserve.

adults, exemplified the new generation's goal of obtaining some skilled training. They were employed as office workers in Ljubljana. They came home
regularly for weekends and tried to help as much as possible with the chores,
both from a sense of loyalty to their parents and as an expression of love for
the village. They no longer wore peasant garb but sleek jeans, t-shirts,
blouses, and city shoes; and as they appeared in their parents' simple farm
house Marija and Tončka represented all that stood for modernity in their
behavior, dress, and outlook. Although they realized that their parents were
overburdened by having to do all the farm labor alone, they clearly would not
consider changing their way of life. Nor did their parents, who were proud of
their childrens' achievements, urge them to. During our last two visits to
Žerovnica my husband and I saw a very welcoming but tired Anton and
Marija trying their best to hold the farm together since Matija Rok and his
wife had died. They expressed some resentment of the few who already used
their connections with the *občina* to establish bed-and-breakfasts. We heard
later that after their mother's death both daughters returned home to help.

The Rok family's boundaries of internal space hardly coincided with any
official demarcations, for within them lay far-off Hibbing in northern Minnesota where Matija Rok's sister, Marija Lunka, lived with her husband,
both born in Žerovnica. We visited her in 1976 in her small, ranch-style

house on a typical midwestern small town residential street. She was as welcoming and as hospitable as her brother, whom she strongly resembled. She was old and frail, and yet lively and spry. There were juxtaposed the modern house, the Slovene American woman, and a pitchfork (*motyka*) Marija Lunka had brought with her from her former home in Žerovnica. In Hibbing this peasant tool hung on the living room wall as its main decorative object, its practical function replaced by aesthetic and emotive ones. There were other mementos of Žerovnica, family photographs and small presents. The home village dominated Marija Lunka's outlook on the world. The hardships she and her husband had faced in their early years in America were still very much alive in her memories, and she talked about them with great feeling. When we returned to Žerovnica in 1992, Tome Primožič told us proudly that she had asked to have the pitchfork buried with her upon her death, "and so it was!"

This narrative of the Rok family exemplifies the effect of point of view on the perception of boundaries and highlights the polysemy and polyfunctionality of objects. It makes concrete what it means to be a culture hero who crosses official boundaries. Self-evaluation of the youth has taken on modern hues: commuting between city and village, these women led a double life.

Anton Debevc and His Family in the Cleveland Area and in Žerovnica

The colorful Anton (Tone) Debevc was born in Žerovnica in 1889. His father was one of the four millers in the village, the group that composed the village's richest segment before the mills were essentially shut down during the communist years. Since younger sons like Anton did not inherit the homestead, they frequently migrated to other villages, cities, or other countries, notably to the United States, and particularly to Cleveland. But Anton Debevc, coming from a more powerful family, was sent to Ljubljana to study for the priesthood. Instead, however, he tried to study medicine through various ingenious ways.

In 1907, at age eighteen, he and a friend left for the United States to avoid Austrian military service. Although he maintained close ties to the village, Anton never returned, about which his nephew, whom I visited in the village, was openly resentful although Anton did send funds to help the family. In contrast, most migrants whose families were impoverished did return for intermittent visits, or permanently, after having gathered some resources for their families. Sometimes their families also joined them in the New World.

Anton went to Cleveland, settling first in the St. Clair Avenue Slovene community and finding work in the steel mills. He also became a *bricoleur* inventor, devising a machine out of old propellers and airplane motors. The contraption, which he patented, could send smoke over vineyards to protect them from frost. In 1916 he bought land outside of Cleveland, built a house, and became a vintner. He invented more machines for his farm to irrigate his vineyards, and kept bees and other animals, as all Žerovnica peasants did. At various times, Anton also served as the local sheriff or an insurance agent, and he founded a Slovene Catholic parish near his farm.

The year after he bought his farm, he married in the traditional Slovene way. A friend from his own village, who lived near his farm outside of Cleveland, acted as a matchmaker, bringing to his house a woman Anton had not previously known but who was born in Grahovo, one kilometer from Žerovnica. He married her in 1917. His wife died in 1973, and he died in the 1980s. At the time of our visits to him in the 1970s, his thirty-six–hectare vineyard was surrounded by the larger vineyards of his four children. They produced the wine from their own and Anton's vineyards. One son owns a wine-tasting restaurant similar to the Slovene *gostilna,* designed to look like a Slovene Alpine inn, where wine and Slovene food is served. While the Debevc farms are not a joint enterprise where all sons share ownership, they recall the post-*zadruga* Slovene family in which, according to the records, each son inherited the land in equal shares. While Anton's landholdings did not match the entire landholdings of his village of origin, they do suggest the village adage often expressed in Žerovnica, "If we went to America, one farm would be the size of all the land of our village!"

Anton remained in close correspondence with his inheriting brother in Žerovnica. He told us in the 1970s that he had sent $1,000 to his brother, and he boasted that he was a millionaire. The joke was that he was a millionaire only in Yugoslav dinars at the latter currency's unfavorable exchange rate. He explained that he sent his brother the money to help him pay off the mortgage for his barn. In keeping with an idealized view of the village, he said the people there were good and honest. No one had ever stolen.

In spite of his long absence, Tone knew a considerable amount about the village. He had heard about the attempts to close the drainage holes of the karstic Cerknica Lake in order to prevent the water from escaping every year. Like all villagers, he predicted that the project to close the sinkholes in the lake would not be successful: "You cannot conquer the lake!"

Many signs of the village surrounded him: the linden (*lipa*) trees he planted and from whose blossoms he made tea; the barn where young men congregated and often spent the night as young village men often did in the village. Anton dressed like a peasant and mostly spoke a somewhat archaic Slovene mixed with English. He looked strikingly like a villager except that he was more robust and vigorous.

In the framework of Lotman's narrative model, Anton was a boundary crosser from his youth on throughout his entire life, and thus a culture hero. Early boundary-crossing events that violated rules of the traditional Slovene village culture included Anton's attempt to study medicine instead of for the priesthood, thereby thwarting the will of his father; and his departure for America, abandoning the priesthood which his father had chosen for him as a profession. The fortitude that these events signified in Anton's consciousness transformed into the daring that initiated more events in the New World.

Thus Anton did not stay long within the confines of the peasant workers' culture of the ethnic, village-like Slovene neighborhood in central Cleveland, but became a commercial farmer, cultivating grapes for the market. At the same time, he became a sheriff, thus joining forces with what is traditionally viewed as part of the oppressive state. He also became a businessman selling insurance. Additionally, he was an inventor and obtained patents for his inventions, not just a peasant *bricoleur*. Yet this eventful life included traditional village ways as well: a marriage arranged by a matchmaker to a strange woman from a neighboring Slovene village; the *zadruga*-like farm arrangement in Ohio in which four sons cooperated; and the strong attachment to, and feelings of responsibility for, the older brother in Žerovnica whom Anton had not seen since he was 18.

I now turn to specific montage elements related to the figure of Anton. The visual impact of Anton Debevc, the nature of his discourse, his peasant clothes (from the beat-up fedora hat to the rubber boots), his lack of teeth so typical of all village elders, his apologies for being just a poor farmer although he was in fact quite successful, are traditional elements that contrast with his adoption of Americanized behavior and characteristics such as his robust appearance, his hurried gate, his frequent laughter, his boisterous jokes, all at variance with the more sober and restrained typical Slovene villager. The picture of Anton in peasant garb, utilizing traditional gestures as he is seated on a large tractor seen only on state farms in the homeland presents the observer with a range of juxtapositions. He also told us that he never ate anything but traditional Slovene food grown by himself, despite the fact that he owned a large-scale farm.

All these qualities defy the less dominant aspect of his personality: the modest but stubborn and tough traditional peasant villager who exhibits ingenuity. Anton the culture hero suggests the actor in an epic tale, the crosser of many boundaries at once; he is a superman, he is never sick, and no feat is too hard for him.

The following examples of Anton's discourse and behavior demonstrate his multiple roles:

THE UNCONQUERABLE CULTURE HERO

"I am the first Slovene farmer here."

"I'm a millionaire." (joke; "only in Yugoslav dinars")

"I've never lost a crop." (Points to his head) "This cabbage is smart." "I'm foxy."

"My eyes are smart. I never need glasses."

"Bees never sting me." (He acts out his method of controlling the queen and getting honey, protecting himself with vinegar.)

"I am never sick, never tired, and never cold." (Exhibits his warm hands in cold weather although ours are cold) "I have good circulation."

"I do all my own work. I work fast. I don't need anyone. I even argue with myself. Before you start to think about something, I make it. If you stop work, you die. I never lose time: I work in the fields all winter. I take cheese in my pockets, no lunch. I can do anything." (Tells of incredible exploits as sheriff.) "I help everyone. My door is always open."

THE MYTHOLOGICAL INVENTOR AND SHAMAN

"Haven't you read about me in the papers?" "I could go to the moon with my inventions." "I could take the engine out of your car and use it" (jokingly threatens to do so). "I only use old parts."

His shaman-like healing abilities are demonstrated by his special knowledge. "I know how to stay strong and never get sick. I only eat pure food and use pure fertilizer."

He names the Slovene crops he grows and what he eats: turnips (*repa*), beets (*pesa*), *žgance*, fried corn mush (*polenta*), potatoes (*krompir*), buckwheat (*ajda*), meat and milk from his own farm. "I know how to make medicine from plants, and tea from the *lipa* tree. I grow garlic for flu. I learned all this from the Slovene priest. I operated on myself, removed a blood clot in my arm" (shows us the scar). "I know everything because I am wise and old."

In sum, all the above characteristics of Anton Debevc, from the unconquerable hero to the *bricoleur* shaman, are counterposed to Anton's traditional qualities, loyalty to the church, devotion to his village, fulfillment of brotherly obligations, attachment to Slovene customs and language, modesty and simple clothes. Anton used to play the button box, the traditional peasant instrument, which hints at his mediating role. Together all these elements structurally interrelate in the plot-like life story of Anton Debevc. In Victor Turner's sense Anton is a performance in a social drama.

Anton, the dominant member of the extended human sign also includes a network of family members in Žerovnica and in Geneva, Ohio, near Anton's farm. On our last visit to Žerovnica in 1995, after the fall of communism, I visited Ivan Debevc, one of the millers, the son of Anton's deceased brother. Ivan Debevc was resentful because his uncle had never returned for a visit, while Anton's son, also Anton (Tone), who owned the winery did visit, as did Anton's daughter, Julia Grabelšek. But Ivan recalled that Anton had written that he wanted to come home and fix up the sawmill. But he never did. Ivan's wife showed us a letter from Julia Grabelšek that was lying in the top drawer of a dresser in the kitchen. Julia writes frequently. She also runs a winery similar to her brother's, but on a smaller scale. Ivan presented us with two baskets that he had woven. One was for my husband and me, and one for his cousin Julia, and he asked us to give it to her when we returned to Cleveland.

Ivan complained about the village economy. There was not enough water for the mills so they had to use expensive electric power. As long as Yugoslavia existed, there had been a market for village products. But these markets in the other former Yugoslav republics had now vanished. Furthermore, the pensions for people who did not work at Brest but only on their land were very small. These were only a few recent innovations for peasants, and the issue of pensions was a stormy one.

Pursuing the network, I returned to the Cleveland area a few months later and visited Julia Grabelšek. I also met Julia's twin sister, whose personality contrasted sharply with Julia's. In every way the two sisters differed. Julia's leitmotif was: "I'm very ethnic." Her personality recalled that of her father. She was full of pep, bubbling over. She took care of her father after his wife had died. She had a big vineyard on which she did all the work alone. At the time of our visit in 1995 she was in her seventies. Her husband had died. To her, a *kozolec* that she planned to build on her farm, conveyed nostalgia. She also wanted to erect an *ostrv*, a simpler structure for drying crops that is really only a high vertical pole stuck in the ground. She related the story of the bell she brought back to her father from his brother's mill in Žerovnica in 1964. When her father heard the sound of the bell, he cried. For the sound reminded him of the Žerovnica sawmill where the bell announced that a log had passed the circular saw. She also had brought a miniature piece of log track from the Žerovnica mill, and a beet grater from the village. She frequented antique sales to look for old tools that reminded her of Žerovnica, and she constantly returned to her wish to build a *kozolec*, pointing to a place on her property where it would stand. I showed her the UNESCO publication about the *kozolec*, and she leafed through it with great interest. She told us that she had nothing against the Slovene group that came to Cleveland from European displaced persons camps after 1950, a group whose picnic grounds are located right across the river from her land, and which are marked by a large concrete *kozolec*. She recalled that before the river banks became overgrown, she would sit and watch the activities and listen to the music coming from the recreational lands. When they would stop playing the harmonica, she would answer and tease them by playing her own harmonica, although she claimed not very well.

She believed that the younger generation who speaks little Slovene, as for example her own daughter, were curious about their past, and she implied that this was a reaction against their formerly ignoring it: "Now they want to know." She described the world around her father's farm in the following manner: Her father was generous, gave grape juice away, and did not always collect money owed to him. She continued that her father took the street car to Madison, Ohio as a young man. When he got off in Madison, he just started walking. He had $3,000 in his pocket. When he came to a place where people wanted to sell a farm of 80 acres with a house, he bought it on the spot. The son of the sellers was retarded and set fire to the house after the Debevc family had moved in. The insurance refused to pay because the house burned down so shortly after the contract. One thousand dollars in cash lying in a drawer inside the house had also burned up. Although his wife wanted him to give up, Anton felled some trees and within a short time had rough-hewn walls ready and continued building while he and his wife lived in the barn. He collected old tin cans from the town dump and boiled milk on an outdoor fire. The can melted and milk spilled. So they ate apples. Even upon completion the house remained rough hewn, but, Julia commented, "what fun we had in it and what a nice family life we had!" There were always guests. People would come from Cleveland for weekends and have picnics. Anton never charged them. As Julia said, "We may not have been as rich as some, but dad had more friends than anyone because he was so hospitable and always gave things away. They had no water or modern plumbing in the house until the 1920s."

Julia said that her father never went back to Žerovnica because he believed that he had to be back the same evening to do chores, although he always used to say: "I'll go for one day and come back in the evening and do chores."

Concerning the traditional St. Clair neighborhood, Julia thought that the older generation would not leave their houses. She knew someone who sold a house in the neighborhood and received $5,000 because the area was deteriorating. And she said, "If I had a house there, I would stay. I would just live differently and not go out at night." At the same time, she claimed to be an outdoor person who had difficulties remaining inside. She concluded that "everything is upside down since dad passed away."

Here then we have the story of an intercommunicating network composed of Anton on his farm outside Cleveland, his daughters and sons living close by, Anton's farm, Anton's brother—although dead very much alive in Anton's memory—Anton's nephew in Žerovnica, and the many meaningful objects and memories that circulated between them.

A Wonderful Father, a Daughter, and a Close Companion

The following narrative is based on data drawn from conversations with an elderly Slovene American woman taped in 1976. Anna Jakšič was a widow then in her eighties and blind. Born in 1894 in a small Slovene town near Žerovnica, she was brought to Cleveland by her mother as a small child. They were following her father who had arrived a few years earlier. At the time of my study, Anna still lived in her spacious family home on St. Clair Avenue with her companion, Marija, who was born in Žerovnica. Anna, a member of the Grdina family, was among the leaders of the traditional Slovene community. Anna compensated for her blindness to make it hardly noticeable.

The middle-aged Marija was the only member of her immediate family who had come to the United States, while Anna's father had come with his three brothers. Marija never married and took on the traditional role of the *teta*, the unmarried aunt in the large Slovene peasant family. Anna had nine sisters and brothers in the United States, four children of her own, and many grandchildren. Anna and her husband followed in the Grdina tradition of her father and his three brothers who all became strong leaders of the community. They embodied many traditional virtues and proved inventive and boundary-crossing in the new environment.

Anna's father had died in 1922, her mother in 1945. Her father and his brothers had not been peasants but had worked as hatmakers, artisans, and traders in Slovenia; they also were musicians. They traveled from market to market selling their wares and putting on singing performances. They arrived in the United States with no funds, but with more training than the typical Slovene peasant migrant, which gave them a significant advantage over the average peasant immigrants. The group first went to the Pennsylvania mines; then they moved to a hat factory in Cleveland. They soon began to acquire first stores, then saloons and boardinghouses, and finally a newspaper business.

In her childhood, Anna worked in her parents' store and saloon. In 1914 she married a successful Slovene cabinetmaker. Anna lives in a comfortable and spacious apartment located over the store once owned by her parents. Mementos of Slovenia abounded. Anna's self-image is clearly that of an aristocratic leader among the older generation of Slovene immigrants who believe that they have a strong obligation to those left behind in Slovenia. When she visited Slovenia in the late 1930s, the poverty and hospitality she observed only strengthened her and her husband's activities in the United States.

Marija's story is simpler. She arrived in America at fourteen years of age and, at the time of our visit, was in her sixties. She always worked hard and remained attached to her village, to which she had returned much as a child. She believes little has changed in Žerovnica and sees the Cleveland Slovene district itself as very much like a Slovene village. We might say in Lotman's metaphor of traditional types that she remained part of the structure, never mentally crossing a boundary. In contrast we may look to Anna as a Lotmanian culture hero, a bold boundary-crosser.

The following list contrasts the positive Slovene traditional values which signal Anna's self-identity as opposed to devalued negative oppositions. Thus, representing the traditional culture, I note the following oppositions on the axis from good to bad:

1 reciprocity, cooperation, and help/nonreciprocity, noncooperation, and nonhelp;
2 hospitality/inhospitality;
3 generosity/stinginess;
4 respect for elders, patriarchal authority, and kin/disregard of traditional family ties;
5 work for family or community/work for egotistical ends;
6 play, gaiety, music, dramatic and carnival behavior/dreariness;
7 stubbornness, beating the game, bravery, peasant ingenuity/withdrawn behavior, lack of humor;
8 toughness/docility, cowardice, naïveté;
9 epic culture hero, crosser of boundaries/lack of imagination, obedience.

As an excellent raconteur, Anna fashions her conversations into performances of a sort. While she sits at the head of a formal dining room table talking, Marija serves ample food and drink. The setting itself is a highly polysemic text. The dining room opens into a well furnished living room, adorned with photographs, old books, and memorabilia. Personal records, newspaper clippings, old costumes, and other objects supporting Anna's tales, are retrieved for us from the attic. Marija's echo-like support punctuates Anna's comments. Anna's memory is strong and, in spite of her blindness, highly visual. She frequently remarks, "I remember this very well. I still see it now." She fills her narration with direct quotations and repeats certain generalities over and over again. In carefully traditional dress she keeps a controlled formal posture. Her hospitality is dignified but insistent, and all of this contrasts with the more relaxed and informal American mode. The following characteristic may be idiosyncratic, but convey the typical Slovene peasant's courage in the face of obstacles: Anna does not project her blindness as a handicap. In fact, she appears to see more than most people in spite of it.

Anna's personality is expressed most vividly in her stories about "Father" or "Daddy" who constitutes the strongest part of her self-identity although she also identified with her mother. I classify Anna and her parents in Lotman's terms as culture heroes. From Anna's remarks, I characterize her parents in the following way: "Daddy" is a culture hero, a crosser of boundaries par excellence whose personality encompasses all the traditional values of Slovene culture we have spoken of before. In contrast, "Mother," although in some ways similar to "Father," comes across in Anna's narrative as the less adventurous, more businesslike person who does not delight in travel and change as much as "Daddy" does.

Anna's father had a complex character. When he arrived in Pennsylvania he came into conflict with the German and Irish workers, had a brutal fight, and was thrown into a ditch, after which he said to himself "I am going to Cleveland." When he arrived there, he found a job in Johnson's straw hat factory. But when he observed the work there, he told his bosses, "This is not the way to do it. You should know how. You don't just cut and take a piece and then start to sew it. You need a block for a hat." So in 1920 they sent him to New York with a German interpreter, because "Daddy" spoke German, and had blocks made to his specifications. Upon his return he found many Slovenes to work for Johnson's, and soon he became superintendent. He always found work for newly arriving Slovenes at Johnson's or other nearby factories. He also provided boarding for them and was known never to turn anyone away.

"Daddy" 's hard work and his ability to make hats is counterposed to his "gypsy blood" that signals his lighter side. Anna recalls, "We always said there was gypsy blood in my parents because they were always playing or bumming around. I remember a friend who had been a student in Slovenia who said, 'I'll never forget your parents. When I was a student, they came to sell their hats and they always would sing, and they always sold their merchandise before anybody else because they sang while selling.'" Marija then recalled village fairs in Žerovnica in the church on the hill, acting as a kind of chorus to Anna's remarks.

The following events in Anna's childhood also support the playful and imaginative side of "Daddy"'s personality. Anna recalled, "I remember so well about the woodshed. I see it now. The woodshed had coal in it, and it burned down. When it burned down, that evening we had a potato roast outside. Mother was upset. All that old lumber to clean away. So Daddy made a party out of it—a bonfire and a potato roast. And Mother said, 'You make a party out of everything that happens.' Dad answered, 'Well, we've gotta clean the place up anyhow, so if we have a party maybe more people will clean it up than otherwise.'" Yet "Father" also upheld the more conservative personal traditions such as loyalty to kin. In the ethnic situation, his generosity stretched from kin and village to ethnic Slovenes in Cleveland in general. As Anna reported, "Dad said everybody should help one another. You never questioned what you were going to get for it. You're just going to help that man until he gets a job."

Anna recalled that once a young Slovene woman came to her father's house. She was the daughter of a peasant in Slovenia and had seen a calendar of the funeral parlor that was run by Anna's father's brother. (Similar calendars from the Grdina funeral home decorated many village houses in Slovenia during my visits, condensed signs that related Cleveland to Žerovnica. Anna continued, "The girl arrived in Cleveland with the calendar and went to see Uncle Tony. Uncle Tony brought her to my mother and said, 'I have nothing but boys; Ma you take her, I can't keep her.' So she stayed with us that night, and she stayed with us until she got married, and she became one of our boarders."

The traditional theme of the helping and generous father is constantly repeated. As Anna tells it, "I remember when I was about eight years old, Daddy said, 'Well, I'm going to sleep on the floor today,' because people would take our beds. The next day he said, 'Well, where are you from?' and then he found someone who would give this person a job." Yet further facets constituted the father's ethnic identity. Anna observed: "Daddy always said, 'You've gotta become a citizen, and you've gotta join the lodge [the Slovene Cooperative Society] so in case you die you've got somebody to bury you.'"

Anna also related the well-known story of an expedition to California in search of gold led by a priest who defrauded the Slovene Clevelanders. In 1897, shortly after "Father" had settled in the hat factory on St. Clair Avenue, he took part in the California trip to search for gold. Anna remembers that about 100 people got together, pooled their money, and were led by the local priest to start a new colony in California. The trip failed, and the priest was said to have drowned. The California story, the search for a pot of gold, an odyssey of the adventurer who conquers all obstacles in the search for a hidden treasure, but, as in this case, fails, is associated with many remembered events related to Indians and the hard life in the West.

After "Father" returned from California in the early 1900s, he opened up a dry goods store, and eventually Anna's parents had two stores adjoining each other. "Mother" sold ladies' clothing while "Father" offered men's furnishings and employed several workers. However, "Father" sold his store and opened up another store for newspapers in an outlying district; he also became an editor of a newspaper and began to travel. As Anna recalls over and over, somewhere around 1910 or 1912 her father sent a telegram to her mother from Milwaukee, saying, "Sell your store. I've bought a saloon here." So her mother, defying her husband's strictures, went to his brother who had a saloon and said, "Sell me your saloon. Your brother is in Milwaukee buying a saloon, and I certainly don't want to go there." So "Mother" sent a wire: "Come home. I've bought a saloon for you here." Thus began life in the saloon. The parents rented a large building that was owned by a brewery and included a saloon, a dance hall, and a meeting hall; it had enough space to take in a large number of boarders and became a center for dramatic skits and singing, meetings of all kinds, and generally a Slovene center. One can consider it a syncretic institution iconic of the precommunist village firemen's association (*gasilno društvo*), a traditional center for similar activities. The whole family worked hard in this saloon. Anna recalled the structure of the building: "We did not have to go into the saloon; daddy always had a bartender. But we had to take care of the halls. The second floor was the dance hall and alongside it was the banquet hall where weddings were celebrated."

The saloon and California stories describe the adventurous quality of "Father" and mirrors the more restrained courage and humor of the leading villager Matija Rok.

I summarize "Father" as an educator of the children and a model for the family. The following narration depicts three interrelated themes: (1) the work ethic; (2) "Father"'s disciplinary role within the family based on patriarchal authority, particularly in relation to the goal of instilling honesty; and (3) the theme of generosity and hospitality as it was extended to all ethnic Slovenes.

To illustrate the family's work obligations, Anna repeats over and over, "We worked hard. We worked hard," and, "Working will never hurt anybody! We didn't have time to get into trouble." Anna recalled a wedding where she had to clean and do the cooking and that she complained to "Mother" of her tiredness. "Mother" responded: "The music will start. You'll forget how tired you are." Anna remembered that around 1911 there were only three girls left in the house. "So the place was given over to me, see. I was only a kid then, but naturally I had to take charge of the work. You just do it, that's all. When Mother says, 'This is to be done,' it's done." Anna recalled that when she was around thirteen years old, she told her mother that she would take over the store that her parents had to sell at that time due to financial problems. Later another store was bought, and Anna went to study millinery and her sister became a beautician so they could contribute in the store. "Mother said, 'The store is empty. I got nine kids and if they don't go into the business, I'm going to have to go back myself.' Well, that's the last thing we wanted Mother to do."

The following is a more extended comment by Anna about the work program which contrasts in its intensity and discipline with American norms.

> Well, we all worked. As soon as you were thirteen years old, you worked. You had to do something. Well, you just did it, that's all. You went to work. You just did. The first thing that you did in our house as a child, you had to see that the yard was cleaned. That went according to ages, you know. The yard had to be cleaned. Then the shoes were polished by the next oldest. When you were a certain age, you took care of all the shoes that Saturday when you were home. The yard first, then there was the shoes. Each one had a job to do and you had to do it. You didn't have to do it. It wasn't a have-to, it was your job and you did it.

This story recalls the neat Slovene villages, with well-kept yards and strict standards pertaining to clothes and appearance, all signaling pride in self and village. Anna continued, "When you were older and you were a girl, you worked on your trousseau. Mother never let anybody get married without having her trousseau."

Discipline and honesty were village values strictly instilled in the ethnic situation.

I was five years old and I wanted a doll. There was a candy store on St. Clair where I used to get Daddy tobacco because he chewed tobacco. They had a doll hanging there, I see it now. And I wanted that doll so bad, so I went and I "snitched" a nickel and I bought the doll. By the time I came home my parents knew about it. "Where were you?" I said, "Oh, I don't know." I wouldn't tell them about the doll. Mother said, "Did you buy something? Did you buy a doll?" I must have said yes. "Where did you get the money?" "I found it." "You must have taken it," Mother said. So I confessed that I took it. Mother said, "You know you didn't find it. No nickels are to be found. So you take the doll back to Lindenmann's Store and tell them to give you the nickel and you bring the nickel to us."

Anna told another story referring to discipline:

I'll never forget, my brother did something. I don't know what. Dad put us all around on chairs. We all sat in one room right across from the store. There were two steps up and then it was like in our living room, and we all had to sit around, the whole family. And Daddy said to me, "Go and get the stick." I said, "No, I don't want to," and he said, "Then I'll give it to you." This was the only time we got spanked, and we all cried.

She also noted, "If we came home late from a dance, Daddy always said, 'You must have swept up the hall.' He said this because the last one to leave always sweeps up the hall."

Another visually depicted drama exemplifies traditional morality instilled by the father:

Daddy would always walk through the saloon and when he walked through and came back he would always light a match, explaining, "I'm going to feed the dog in the alley." But he was really checking on the girsl [people who were working for the family in the saloon]. He was a wonderful father. I'll never forget him. He always said, "If there's going to be girls in the house, I don't want shame in the house. I don't want blame for anything."

Turning to the theme of hospitality and generosity, Anna told us that there were parties, singing, and balls of all kinds. When Anna was a child and her parents had stores, people came there to buy clothes for weddings, and, as she recalls, they always said, "You're coming to the wedding. Don't forget the girls who work in your store. They always come and sing Slovene songs." Her father believed the Lojzar girls (a pseudonym) made the weddings so successful, but he and his wife would also perform duets during the celebration.

Costume balls and old-fashioned parties of all kinds were always organized at the spur of the moment. Anna painted the following scene:

> When I was a child, after school, at four o'clock every afternoon, there always was a pot of coffee on the table with some rolls, if nothing else, bread and jelly. The door was always open to everyone. Daddy always said, "You're never so poor that you can't give someone something to eat who comes into our house. Never let anyone leave your house without something to eat."

Anna frequently recalled her trip to Slovenia in 1939. She then finally understood "Daddy" because she saw the people's poverty alongside their generosity. "Life was beautiful." She added another story. "Our Daddy was very good. I remember a doctor. He always said that if it hadn't been for our food and coffee, he wouldn't have been able to get through medical school. People just came—students had plays and rehearsals and then coffee, and we always had homemade bread."

The following scenes illustrate the interrelation of patriarchal authority, honesty, and generosity as exemplified by attitudes toward money. They also exemplify the independence of the father's own morality in the face of community disapproval. Anna recalled,

> We had a lot of help. Daddy had a habit of putting a little money here and there, and if it disappeared you'd know someone took it. He'd leave money all over. We were cleaning in the saloon and I found a cigar box full of money and I went to Mama. "Look at the money." She answered, "Just give it to me. Daddy's putting it aside." He'd throw it in a cigar box. I can remember the place it was. We had fun with our parents. They were tremendous parents.

As this and other tales show, money was a many-leveled complex sign relating to temptation and self-control. It was also a sign of generosity and friendship, and of its opposite, jealousy. The Grdinas were known as being better off than most people, and this aroused jealousy. "But Father used to say, 'If you want to be praised you gotta die. Or if you want them to talk about you, get married, but if you want them to praise you, die.' " And that was how he handled the problem of jealousy.

"Father" is remembered as being almost mythically generous. The following story demonstrates that money was not simply to be kept for personal power. Rather it was to be distributed.

> Father died in 1922 and we found his ledger. We couldn't figure it out. It was written like, "Mary (that worked for John), $10.00." "This man that lives at this lady's house, $100.00." There were thousands of dollars in the book, and there were no last names. Daddy gave money, and he was ashamed to ask people what their last name was if he didn't know it. I said to Mother, "What are you going to do with this book?" She said, "Just throw it in the furnace. I'll never collect." Daddy gave away thousands of dollars, but he would never insult anybody by letting him know that he didn't know their last name. But we never missed the money. If you didn't have it, you didn't miss it.

These brief selections underscore that Anna, Marija, Anna's children, and her parents compose an extended human sign text, their actions composing a plot-like narration. Anna is a teller of tales. She invokes action and images as she dramatizes them herself by carrying out hospitality rites in a setting where such rites strongly suggest traditional Slovenia as well as the traditional ethnic neighborhood on St. Clair Avenue. When juxtaposed to non-Slovene Cleveland, it has the quality of an explicit montage. Anna and "Mother" are also culture heroes, innovative and independent, and crossers of boundaries. "Mother" buys a saloon without her husband's knowledge. Anna offers to take over the store at age thirteen. She becomes a community leader in spite of her blindness. The entire text is placed in the context of Anna's ethnic neighborhood, itself part of urban, industrial Cleveland where ethnic conflict and urban sprawl are endemic to the surrounding communities.

Chapter Eight

Concluding Remarks

The Village and the Ethnic Community

Considering the semiotic portraits of villagers and ethnic Slovenes, there is much to compare between Mary Molek's perception and description of her mother, Ivan Molek's reflexive self-portrait, Anton Debevc's relationships with his family, Anna Jakšič's relation to her parents and to Marija, and Matija Rok's attitude toward his family in Žerovnica and Hibbing. There are both affinities and oppositions between these four groups which dramatize the complexities of the meaning of transnationalism.

As I have shown, recent decades have brought radical changes to both communities. After Slovenia won its independence, Žerovnica turned to tourism and the ensuing essential abandonment of the elders who are barely aided on weekends by commuting adult offspring. This situation has led to the decline of traditional field cultivation and to that of the formerly well-kept village. But the change also brings upward mobility to the youth as they begin increasingly to become semiskilled and skilled workers in the cities. Yet they maintain their allegiance to the village and all the associated nostalgic recollections. However, the poorer peasants and elders cannot take great comfort in the regulations that protected the architectural uniformity of the village.

In contrast, there was no official concern or aid for the preservation of the ethnic Slovene traditional urban neighborhood bounded by St. Clair Avenue. Rather, the upward mobility of the second and third generations parallels the new life of the younger generation in Žerovnica. Yet the younger generation who now lives in the suburbs exhibits a strong desire to visit the village. Both young and old now seem to hold emotional attachments to the village and to the once vibrant St. Clair Avenue ethnic community. Indeed, the ethnic community used its greater resources to help preserve Slovene customs and way of life by supporting the Slovene National Homes and their programs. Also well supported were the protected farm lands. In both Žerovnica and Cleveland the traditional core of the community has been eroding. But while the elders were protected in the ethnic community, they were not in Žerovnica. Today Slovene associations and activities are carried on in a middle-class American setting. The solution for the ethnic Slovene elders, their special institutions such as retirement homes and nursing homes, reflect the strength of the American economy but also the preservation of Slovene norms.

Interrelations between the Žerovnica and Cleveland continue but have undergone transformations. Ethnic Slovenes visit Žerovnica bringing with them lost traditions, a more critical perspective on America, and a more positive one on Slovenia, Slovenes visit their relatives in the USA, but they no longer think of immigration as the answer.

In conclusion to the discussion of semiotic portraits, I note the circularity of the dialogue from one continent to another, the effect of poverty on the village and on the early lives of the immigrants, and the ironic reversals of the fate of the elders in the village and in the ethnic setting. It speaks to both the vulnerability and strength of ways of life exposed to the force of modernization, power, immigration, and transnationalism.

Sequel: The Elusive Nostalgia

Jakobson held that Peirce's Symbol or Legisign (which are the fundamental manifestations of Peirce's Third) compose the essential difference between human and nonhuman forms of communication (1952, 565). Furthermore, Peirce's Third and closely related concepts such as Crapanzano's authoritative function, Uspensky's semantic dominant, Bakhtin's dialogue and heteroglossia, Lotman's concept of cultural explosion (the view that gradual change is only one aspect of change while explosion is the other), and Wolf's broad interpretation of the concept of ideas' context and history are all wellsprings of human culture and creativity that may give birth to power and domination. Inversely, culture texts may be preservative since nostalgia lurks within them. The dynamism of human culture tells us that much is unpredictable and related to chance and that cultural traditions do not disappear. In the face of overwhelming odds, some values must give way and be replaced by new ones, although the traditional way of life is still remembered. It appears that memory cannot be easily erased.

Using nostalgia as our guide in rethinking these various narratives, we find an idea expressed and reexpressed. In Žerovnica nostalgia has a strong hold on everyday life. The sound of threshing may remind villagers of an earlier atmosphere of collective activities, for example. Earlier times are often described as celebratory and gay, inscribed with greater autonomy and solidarity. "Today we have no times for such activities," villagers commonly observed during the communist era. But while the postcommunist period has freed them from many restrictions, the isolation, particularly of elders, has left a feeling of resignation (despite the reintroduction of the popular carnival, for example).

Nostalgia was also a linking theme in the works of the semiotically oriented thinkers discussed here. Bakhtin's work in many respects presents a play on forms of nostalgia as well as irony and humor. Lotman and Uspensky's joint work on the semiotics of Russian history and the poetics of everyday behavior and Uspensky's work on the semiotics of history attempt to rescue history and memory with all their nostalgic nuances. Bahloul's study of Sephardic Jews who emigrated from Algiers to France is a powerful testament to the force of nostalgia. Hofer's *Latent Ethnicity* tells us that one cannot separate ethnicity and nostalgia.

I return now to Wolf's critique of the view of "society" (or by implication "nation" or "state") that sets up such entities as "eternal verities" or the "timeless essence" of individuals (1980, 760). In this study I agree with Wolf, highlighting the vacuousness of such positions. Thus I have traced the ever-changing relations between the larger society and the villager, as well as their volatile interpenetration, and the interconnections between the diasporic community primarily in Cleveland and the home village. I have stressed "nostalgia," which I find permeates the sensibilities of the migrants and the villagers themselves, and the many ways these remembrances are communicated, Nostalgia is also played upon and manipulated by the larger society and has today become harnessed to the world of tourism.

Thus this book tells a story of communication between asymmetrical partners at home and abroad. It becomes clear that changing dynamics defy simple cause-and-effect and that strict static structuralism and binarity or crass empiricism bear only partial truths. All must accommodate Thirdness, a theme in Herzfeld's *Cultural Intimacy* (1997). While Peirce tells us that twoness exists in every set, without Thirdness, it is not complete. Thus this narrative demonstrates that, while we may reject the postmodern collapse, we cannot return to earlier simplifications or reifications of the past. Here I take the liberty of quoting from an earlier study of mine. "The tensions, conflicts and interrelations between urban elites . . . are one of the fundamental and interacting oppositions characterizing cultural systems since the Neolithic. The character of such interrelations is largely dependent upon context. For only in specific contexts can we interpret, for example, the aesthetic productions of peasants and urban artists as interpenetrating structures" (1984, 131). Indeed, creative and imaginative peasants, innovative migrant adventurers, rebels and carriers of rich cultural traditions are vibrant examples of Peirce's Third. In spite of Peirce's abduction, which is powerful yet permeated by folk beliefs, we must accept some uncertainty and indeterminancy in our interpretations of cultural behavior and in the complex communications and transformations of meanings, whether conscious or subliminal, that arise.

Notes

1   For discussions of the early history of semiotics, see Todorov 1978, 1–42 and Holenstein 1976, 42–67.
2   All references to Peirce are given in the traditional format. Thus CP 2.305 means *Collected Papers,* vol. 2, paragraph 305.

Chapter One   A Glance at the Village and Its Sister Communities in Cleveland and Hibbing

1   *Balina* is a southern European game related to bowling. Its Italian counterpart is *boccia,* and the French variant is called *boules.*
2   The Cerknica Lake, because of its limestone foundation and karstic drainage holes, drains itself in the summer, and in fall the lake begins to fill up again. It is called the drying-up-lake (*zasichajoče jezero*). Its mysteries are now understood, as chapter 5 explains.
3   *Zemlja* literally means "land" or "soil." It is also a land measurement, and one *zemlja* equals sixty hectares.
4   *Zemljak,* a derivative of *zemlja,* means a peasant who owns one *zemlja* of land. A "quarter *zemljak,*" literally a quarter "lander," is a peasant who owns a quarter *zemlja.*
5   I am indebted to Rado Lenček for information concerning non-Slovene minorities in Slovenia.
6   The terms *gospodar* (m.) and *gospodinja* (fem.) designate the head of the family or household.

Chapter Four   Semiotics of Culture

1   I note American anthropologists interested in various semiotic concepts, only some of whom are briefly discussed throughout this study. The following have been primarily interested in Jakobson: Caton (1985, 1987, 1991), Herzfeld (1985 1987, 1991), Urban (1985, 1988), Fernandez (1986, 1991), Bauman (1977), Hymes (1964, 1978, 1996), and Friedrich (1979, 1996a, 1996b). The influence of Peirce is most evident in Singer's many works, in Parmentier (1985a, 1985b, 1985c, 1987), who has worked extensively on Peirce, and in Daniel (1984) who has attempted to apply Peircean schemes

to the Tamil. A number of anthropologists including those linguistically oriented and interested in a text theory that directly or indirectly suggests the Moscow-Tartu School include Hanks (1989) and Geertz (1973b). Mertz and Parmentier have edited a volume on semiotics (1985) that includes Wertsch on Vygotsky and Bakhtin as well as other semiotically oriented articles. Bakhtin's world was an interesting presence in the work of Crapanzano (1990, 1992a, 1992b, 1992c), Marcus (1986, 1992, 1993), Clifford (1986), and others writing in similar modes.

2   Peirce's Legisign and Symbol are both conventional or essentially arbitrary signs. A Legisign is by its nature a law (Peirce uses Law and Rule interchangeably). "A Symbol is a sign which refers to the Object that it denotes by virtue of a 'law' usually an association of several ideas" (CP 2.449). "Any ordinary word as 'give,' 'bird,' 'marriage' is an example of a Symbol and a Legisign" (CP 2.298). "Every Symbol is necessarily a Legisign" (CP 8.335).

A Symbol and a Legisign act through replicas (the Legisign and replica are often referred to as type and token). The Legisign and Symbol and Argument are Thirds. While the Argument is always a Symbol, no sign is without some indexical and Iconic qualities, thus not entirely arbitrary. "Not only does Thirdness suppose and involve the ideas of Secondness and Firstness, but never will it be possible to find any Secondness or Firstness in the phenomenon that is not accompanied by Thirdness" (CP 5.90).

I should note that a Symbol for Peirce differs from that of Cassirer, whose Symbol is largely iconic. Turner's use is closer to that of Cassirer.

3   Here Jakobson overlooked the Interpretant and retained the Saussurean dichotomy signifier/signified but identified the signifier with the object, while Saussure did not (since the signified remained a mental image for him). If Jakobson had involved the interpretant, I believe that his Artifice could emerge from Peirce's degenerate signs, which I am analyzing in a work now in progress. Nevertheless, the Artifice placed in context is a very useful concept.

Chapter Five   Žerovnica: Its Past and the Question of the Future

1   Plural of požiralnik from "*požirativ*," "to swallow up," "to devour." The noun "*požiralnik*" signifies anything that rapidly swallows something, e.g., esophagus, gullet, and, in this case, a karstic sink hole.

2   The word *zadruga* literally means a community or a cooperative. It is also used to describe the traditional South Slavic joint family.

3   *Kuhinja* literally means kitchen. In Žerovnica the word is used to denote the special stove for cooking pig feed.

4   The folk tales and the tale in the following section but not the comparative analysis of the origin of the lake were reported in Portis-Winner 1971.

5   *Nix*—colloquial German negative; *figl fajgl*—an onomatopoetic phrase imitating the sound of sharpening scythes; *durch mahaj*—Slovenized imperative of the German verb *durchmachen*—to carry something through to the end, to complete a task.

6   I am indebted to the late Conrad Arensberg for a personal communication in which he called my attention to these observations that convey the multifunctional and polysemic notion of the number twelve.

7   Since our most recent visit, a second son, Klemen, was born.

8   Hypocoristic form of Jože (Joseph).

9   Postojna is the largest nearby town, about thirty kilometers from Žerovnica.

Chapter Six   The Story of the Ethnic Community in Cleveland

1   For a detailed description of Slovene activities in Cleveland see Susel 1993.

Selected Bibliography

Adorno, Theodor W. and Max Horkheimer. 1986. *Dialectic of Enlightenment.* London: Verso.

Anderson, Benedict. 1983. *Imagined Communities: Reflections on the Origin and Spread of Nationalism.* London: Verso.

Appadurai, Arjun. 1988. "Place and Voice in Anthropological Theory." *Cultural Anthropology* 3.1:16–20.

Arensberg, Conrad M., and Solon T. Kimball. 1965. *Culture and Community.* New York: Harcourt, Brace & World.

Arnez, John A. 1958. *Slovenia in European Affairs: Reflections on Slovenian Political History.* New York: New York League of CSA.

Ashley, David. 1990. "Habermas and the Completion of the Project of Modernity." In *Theories of Modernity and Postmodernity.* Ed. Bryan S. Turner. London: Sage.

Auty, Phyllis. 1965. *Yugoslavia.* London: Thames and Hudson.

Bahloul, Joëlle. 1993a. "Remembering the Domestic Space: A Symbolic Return of Sephardic Jews." In *Going Home.* Ed. Jack Kugelmass. Evanston: Northwestern Univ. Press.

———. 1993b. "Jewish Quarters in Western Europe: The Urban Aesthetics of Identity." Paper presented at meeting of the American Anthropological Association, Washington, D.C. 1993.

———. 1996. *The Architecture of Memory: A Jewish-Muslim Household in Colonial Algeria, 1937–1962.* New York: Cambridge Univ. Press.

Bailey, R. W., L. Matejka, and P. Steiner, eds. 1978. *The Sign: Semiotics around the World.* Ann Arbor: Michigan.

Bakhtin, M. M. 1968. *Rabelais and His World.* Cambridge, Mass.: MIT Press.

———. 1981. *The Dialogic Imagination: Four Essays.* Austin: Univ. of Texas Press.

———. 1990. *Art and Answerability: Early Philosophical Essays.* Austin: Univ. of Texas Press.

———. 1992. *Speech Genres and Other Late Essays.* Austin: Univ. of Texas Press.

Baran, Henryk, ed. 1976. *Semiotics and Structuralism: Readings from the Soviet Union.* White Plains, N.Y.: International Arts and Sciences Press.

———. 1998. "Recepcija Moskovsko-tartuskoj školy v SŠA i Velikobritanii." [The Reception of the Moscow-Tartu School in the USA and Great Britain. In C. Ju. Nekljudov (ed.) *Moskovsko-tartusskaja semiotičeskaja škola. Istorija, vospominanija, razmyšlenija.* [The Moscow-Tartu School of Semiotics. History, Remembrances, Thoughts]. Moscow: The Languages of Russian Culture.

Barnow, Jeffrey. 1986. "Peirce and Derrida: 'Natural Signs' Or Original Trace." *Poetics Today* 7.1:73–94.

Barth, Fredrik. 1979. *Barth by Barth*. New York: Hill & Wang.

——. 1993. *Balinese Worlds*. Chicago: Univ. of Chicago Press.

Barthes, Roland. 1975. "Théorie du texte." In *Encyclopedia universalis*. 7:996–1000. Paris.

Baudelaire, Charles. 1955. *The Mirror of Art: Critical Studies*. London: Phaidon.

Baudrillard, Jean. 1983. *In the Shadow of the Silent Majority*. New York: Semiotext(e).

Baumann, Richard. 1977. *Verbal Art As Performance*. Prospect Heights, Ill.: Waveland Press.

Beaujour, Michel. 1987. "Michel Leiris: Ethnography of Self-Portrayal." *Cultural Anthropology* 2.4:470–78.

Benedict, Ruth. 1948. "Anthropology and the Humanists." *American Anthropologist* 50:585–93.

Benjamin, Walter. 1977. *The Origin of German Tragic Drama*. London: NLB.

Bettelheim, Bruno. 1982. "Reflections (Freud)." *The New Yorker*. March 1:52–93.

Bogatyrev, Petr. 1940. *Lidové divadlo české a slovenské* [Czech and Slovak Folk Theater]. Praha: Borov.

——. 1971. *The Functions of Folk Costume in Moravian Slovakia*. The Hague: Mouton

——. 1976. "Costume As a Sign." In Matejka and Titunik, 13–19.

——. 1982. "A Contribution to the Study of Theatrical Signs." In *The Prague School: Selected Writings, 1929–1946*. Ed. Peter Steiner. Austin: Univ. of Texas Press.

Boissevain, Jeremy., ed. 1993. *Revitalizing European Rituals*. London: Routledge.

Bourdieu, Pierre. 1984. *Distinction: A Social Critique of the Judgement of Taste*. Cambridge, Mass.: Harvard Univ. Press.

——. 1990. *In Other Words: Essays Towards a Reflexive Sociology*. Stanford: Stanford Univ. Press.

——. 1993. "Concluding Remarks: For a Sociogenic Understanding of Intellectual Works." In Calhoun, LiPuma, and Postone, 263–75.

Brady, Ivan, ed. 1991. *Anthropological Poetics*. Savage, Md.: Rowman and Littlefield.

Bricker, Victoria Reifer. 1973. *Ritual Humor in Highland Chiapas*. Austin: Univ. of Texas Press.

Bruner, Edward M. 1984. *Text, Play, and Story: The Construction and Reconstruction of Self and Society.* Washington, D.C.: American Ethnological Society.

——. 1986. "Ethnography As Narrative." In Turner and Bruner 1986.

Bruner, Jerome. 1990. *Acts of Meaning.* Cambridge, Mass.: Harvard Univ. Press.

Buchanan, Allen. 1991. *Secession: The Morality of Political Divorce from Fort Sumter to Lithuania and Quebec.* Boulder: Westview Press.

Bühler, Karl. 1933. *Die Axiomatik der Sprachwissenschaft. Kant Studien* vol. 38.

Calhoun, Craig, Edward LiPuma, and Moishe Postone. 1993. *Bourdieu: Critical Perspectives.* Cambridge: Polity Press.

Carrithers, Michael, Steven Collins, and Steven Lukes, eds. 1985. *The Category of the Person: Anthropology, Philosophy, History.* Cambridge: Cambridge Univ. Press.

Caton, Steven C. 1985. "The Poetic Construction of Self." *Anthropological Quarterly* 58.4:14.

——. 1987. "Contributions of Roman Jakobson." *Annual Review of Anthropology* 16:223–60.

——. 1991. "The 'Voice' of the Despicable: Deviance, Speaking, and Power in Yemeni Tribal Society." In *Deviance: Anthropological Perspectives.* Ed. Morris Freilich, Douglas Raybeck, and Joel Savishinsky. New York: Bergin & Garvey.

Clifford, James. 1983. "Power and Dialogue in Ethnography: Marcel Griaule's Initiation." In *Observers Observed: Essays in Ethnographic Fieldwork.* Ed. George Stocking, Jr. Madison: Univ. of Wisconsin Press. 121–55.

——. 1988. *The Predicament of Culture: Twentieth-Century Ethnography, Literature, and Art.* Cambridge, Mass.: Harvard Univ. Press.

Clifford, James, and George E. Marcus, eds. 1986. *Writing Culture: The Poetics and Politics of Ethnography.* Berkeley and Los Angeles: Univ. of California Press.

Connerton, Paul. 1989. *How Societies Remember.* Cambridge: Cambridge Univ. Press.

Connor, Walker. 1994. *Ethnonationalism: The Quest for Understanding.* Princeton: Princeton Univ. Press.

Čop, J. and Tone Cevc. 1993. *Slovenski kozolec* [The Slovene Hayrack]. Žirovnica (Pot kulturne dediščine).

Corrington, Robert S. 1993. *An Introduction to C. S. Peirce: Philosopher, Semiotician, and Ecstatic Naturalist.* Lanham, Md.: Rowman and Littlefield.

Crapanzano, Vincent. 1990. "Afterword." In Manganaro, 300–308.

——. 1992a. "Self-Characterization." In Crapanzano 1992b, 91–112.

——. 1992b. *Hermes' Dilemma and Hamlet's Desire: On the Epistemology of Interpretation.* Cambridge, Mass.: Harvard Univ. Press.

——. 1992c. "The Postmodern Crisis: Discourse, Parody, Memory." In Marcus, 87–102.

Daniel, E. Valentine. 1984. *Fluid Signs: Being a Person the Tamil Way.* Berkeley and Los Angeles: Univ. of California Press.

Daniel, E. Valentine, and Jeffrey M. Peck, eds. 1996. *Culture/Contexture: Explorations in Anthropology and Literary Studies.* Berkeley and Los Angeles: Univ. of California Press.

Deledalle, Gérard. 1987. *Charles Sanders Peirce: Phénomenologue et sémioticien.* Amsterdam: Benjamins.

——. 1995. "Introduction to Peirce's Semiotic Semiosis." *Semiosis* 79, 80:5–31.

——. 1997. "Peirce and Jakobson: Cross Readings." Paper presented at International Semiotics Symposium in Honor of Thomas G. Winner's Eightieth Birthday.

Derrida, Jacques. 1978. *Writing and Difference.* Chicago: Univ. of Chicago Press.

Docherty, Thomas, ed. 1993. *Postmodernism: A Reader.* New York: Columbia Univ. Press.

Dreyfus, Hubert, and Paul Rabinow. 1993. "Can There Be a Science of Extended Structure and Social Meaning?" In Calhoun, LiPuma, and Postone, 35–44.

Eco, Umberto. 1976a. *A Theory of Semiotics.* Bloomington: Indiana Univ. Press.

——. 1976b. "Peirce and Contemporary Semiotics." *Versus* December: 49–72.

Erlich, Vera St. 1966. *Family in Transition: A Study of 300 Yugoslav Villages.* Princeton: Princeton Univ. Press.

Evans-Pritchard, E. E. 1940. *The Nuer: A Description of the Modes of Livelihood and Political Institution of a Nilotic People.* Oxford: Clarendon Press.

——. 1961. *Anthropology and History: A Lecture Delivered in the University of Manchester with the Support of the Simon Fund for the Social Sciences.* Manchester: Manchester Univ. Press.

Fannigan, Clifford C. 1990. "Liminality, Carnival, and Social Structure." In *Victor Turner and the Construction of Cultural Criticism: Between Literature and Anthropology.* Ed. Kathleen M. Ashley. Bloomington: Indiana Univ. Press. 42–63.

Fanon, Frantz. 1963. *The Wretched of the Earth.* New York: Grove Press.

Fél, Edit, and Tamás Hofer. 1969. *Proper Peasants: Traditional Life in a Hungarian Village.* Chicago: Aldine.

Fél, Edit, Tamás Hofer, and Klarak Csilléry. 1958. *Hungarian Peasant Art.* Budapest: Corvina.

Fernandez, James W. 1986. *Persuasions and Performances: The Play of Tropes in Culture.* Bloomington: Indiana Univ. Press.

———. 1991. *Beyond Metaphor: The Theory of Tropes in Anthropology.* Stanford: Stanford Univ. Press.

Fischer, Michael M. J. 1986. "Ethnicity as Text and Mode." In Marcus and Fischer, 84–96.

Fontaine, J. S. 1985. "Person and Individual: Some Anthropological Reflections." In Carrithers, Collins, and Lukes, 123–140.

Fortes, Meyer. 1945. *The Dynamics of Clanship among the Tallensi: Being the First Part of an Analysis of the Social Structure of a Trans-Volta Tribe.* London: Oxford Univ. Press.

Foucault, Michel. 1961. *Introduction a l'antropologie de Kant.* Université de Paris. Faculté des lettres et des sciences humaines.

———. 1972. *The Order of Things: The Archaeology of Knowledge.* New York: Pantheon.

———. 1980. *Power/Knowledge: Selected Interviews and Other Writings,* 1972–1977. New York: Pantheon.

———. 1987. "What is Enlightenment?" In Rabinow and Sullivan.

Frank, Joseph. 1984. "The Master Linguist." *New York Review of Books* (12 Apr.): 29–33.

Friedrich, Paul. 1979. *Language, Context, and the Imagination.* Stanford: Stanford Univ. Press.

———. 1996a. "The Language of Tragedy and the Tragedy of Language in *Anna Karenina.*" Paper presented at the International Conference on Prague School Linguistics, 70 Years of Existence of the Prague Linguistic Circle and the Hundredth Anniversary of Roman Jakobson's Birthday, Prague, March 28–30, 1996.

———. 1996b. "Culture as Poetry and Poetry as Culture." In Daniel and Peck, 37–57.

Geertz, Clifford. 1973a. *The Interpretation of Cultures: Selected Essays.* New York: Basic Books.

———. 1973b. "Notes on a Balinese Cockfight." In Geertz, 412–53.

———. 1973c. " 'Thick Description': Toward an Interpretative Theory of Culture." In Geertz, 3–30.

———. 1983a. "Blurred Genres: The Refiguration of Social Thought." In Geertz, 19–35.

——. 1983b. "From the Native's Point of View: On the Nature of Anthropological Understanding." In Geertz, 55–70.

——. 1983c. *Local Knowledge: Further Essays in Interpretative Anthropology.* New York: Basic Books.

——. 1995. *After the Fact: Two Countries, Four Decades, One Anthropologist.* Cambridge, Mass.: Harvard Univ. Press.

Gellner, Ernest. 1964. *Thought and Change.* London: Weidenfeld and Nicolson.

Georges, Robert A. 1968. *Studies on Mythology.* Homewood, Ill.: Dorsey.

Gimbutas, Marija. 1971. *The Slavs.* London: Thames and Hudson.

Glazer, Nathan. 1997. *We Are All Multiculturals Now.* Cambridge, Mass.: Harvard Univ. Press.

Glazer, Nathan, and Daniel Patrick Moynihan. 1964. *Beyond the Melting Pot: The Negroes, Puerto Ricans, Jews, Italians, and Irish of New York City.* Cambridge, Mass.: MIT Press.

——. 1973. *Ethnicity and Experience.* Cambridge: Harvard Univ. Press.

Grafenauer, Bogo. 1954–1962. *Zgodovina slovenskega naroda* [History of the Slovene people].

Gruden, J. 1019. *Zgodovina slovenskega naroda* [History of the Slovene People]. Vol. 1. Celovec [Klagenfurt].

Guthrie, W. K. C. 1954. *The Greeks and Their Gods.* Boston: Beacon Press.

Hace, Matevž. 1964. *Tihotapci* [The Smugglers] (novel). Ljubljana: Državna založba.

Halbwachs, Maurice. 1952. *Les cadres sociaux de la mémoire.* Paris: Presses universitaires de France.

——. 1968. *La mémore collective.* Paris: Presses universitaires de France.

Hammel, Eugene A. 1976. "The *zadruga* as Process." In *Household and Family in Past Time: Comparative Studies in the Size and Structure of the Domestic Group over the Past Three Centuries in England, France, Serbia, Japan and Colonial North American with Further Materials from Western Europe.* Ed. Peter Laslett. London: Cambridge Univ. Press.

——. 1993a. "The Yugoslav Labyrinth." *Anthropology of Eastern Europe* (special edition). 11/1–2:35–42.

——. 1993b. "Demography and the Origins of the Yugoslav Civil War." *Anthropology Today* 9:4–9.

Handlin, Oscar. 1990. *The Uprooted.* Boston: Little, Brown.

Hanks, W. F. 1989. "Text and Textuality." *Annual Review of Anthropology* 18:95–127.

Havel, Václav. 1993. "The Post-Communist Nightmare: A Lecture Presented at

George Washington University April 22, 1993." *New York Review of Books* XL(10):8–10.

Hayden, Robert M. 1993. "The Triumph of Chauvinistic Nationalism in Yugoslavia. In Kidecke.

——. 1994. "Meeting the Minotaur." *Anthropology Newsletter* (April): 48.

Herzfeld, Michael. 1985. *Poetics of Manhood: Contest and Identity in a Cretan Mountain Village*. Princeton: Princeton Univ. Press.

——. 1987. *Anthropology through the Looking-Glass: Critical Ethnography in the Margins of Europe*. Cambridge: Cambridge Univ. Press.

——. 1991. *A Place in History: Social and Monumental Time in a Cretan Town*. Princeton: Princeton Univ. Press.

——. 1997. *Cultural Intimacy: Social Poetics in the Nation State*. New York: Routledge.

Hill, Jane H. 1986. "The Refiguration of the Anthropology of Language." *Cultural Anthropology* 1.1:89–103.

Hobsbawm, Eric. 1993a. "Introduction: Inventing Traditions." In Hobsbawm and Ranger, 1–14.

——. 1993b. "Mass-Producing Traditions: Europe 1870–1940." In Hobsbawm and Ranger, 263–307.

Hobsbawm, Eric, and Terence Ranger, eds. 1993. *The Invention of Tradition*. Cambridge: Cambridge Univ. Press.

Hočevar, Toussaint. 1965. *The Structure of the Slovenian Economy, 1848–1963*. New York: Studia Slovenica.

Hofer, Tamás. 1989. "Dramaturgy of the Oppositional Demonstration in Budapest." Lecture presented at the Harvard University Center for European Studies.

——. 1994. *Hungarians between "East and West": National Myths and Symbols*. Budapest: Museum of Ethnography.

——. 1996. "National Schools of European Ethnology and the Question of 'Latent Ethnicity.' *Etnologia Europea* 26:89–96.

Holenstein, Elmar. 1976. *Roman Jakobson's Approach to Language: Phenomenological Structuralism*. Bloomington: Indiana Univ. Press.

Holquist, Michael. 1990. *Dialogism: Bakhtin and His World*. London: Routledge.

Holton, Gerald. 1996. *Einstein, History, and Other Passions: The Rebellion against Science at the End of the Twentieth Century*. Reading, Mass.: Addison-Wesley.

Homans, George Caspar. 1941. *English Villagers of the Thirteenth Century*. Cambridge, Mass.: Harvard Univ. Press.

Hopkins, Gerard Manley. 1959. The *Journals and Papers of Gerard Manley Hopkins*. London: Oxford Univ. Press.

Houser, Nathan, and Christian Kloesel, eds. 1992. *The Essential Peirce: Selected Philosophical Writings*. Bloomington: Indiana Univ. Press.

Hutcheon, Linda. 1988. *A Poetics of Postmodernism: History, Theory, Fiction*. New York: Routledge.

Hymes, Dell. 1962. "The Ethnography of Speaking in Anthropology." In *Anthropology and Human Behavior*. Ed. The Anthropological Society of Washington. Washington, D.C.: The Anthropological Society of Washington. 13–53.

——. 1978. Comments on Soviet Semiotics and Criticism." *New Literary History* 9.2: 399–411.

——. 1996. Equivalence and the Structure of Oral Narrative." Paper presented at the International Conference on Prague School Linguistics, 70 Years of Existence of the Prague Linguistic Circle and Hundredth Anniversary of Roman Jakobson's Birthday, Prague, March 28–30, 1996.

——, ed. 1964. *Language in Culture and Society: A Reader in Linguistics and Anthropology*. New York: Harper and Row.

Innis, Robert E., ed. 1985. *Semiotics: An Introductory Anthology*. Bloomington: Indiana Univ. Press.

——. 1994. *Consciousness and the Play of Signs*. Bloomington: Indiana Univ. Press.

Ivanov, V. V. 1971. "Commentary." 265–95.

——. 1973. "The Category of Time in Twentieth-Century Art and Culture." *Semiotica* 8.1:1–45.

——. 1975. "The Significance of M. M. Bakhtin's Ideas on Sign, Utterance, and Dialogue for Modern Semiotics." *Soviet Studies:* 310–342.

——. 1978. "The Science of Semiotics." *New Literary History* 9.2:189–98.

Ivanov, V. V., and V. M. Toporov. 1976. "The Invariant and Transformation in Folklore Texts." *Dispositio* 3:203–70.

Jakobson, Roman. 1941. "Kindersprache, Aphasie und allegmeine Lautgesetze." In Jakobson 1984. I:329–401.

——. 1952. "Results of a Joint Conference of Anthropologists and Linguists." In Jakobson 1984. II:554–67.

——. 1953a. "Aphasia as a Linguistic Topic." In Jakobson 1984. II:229–38.

——. 1953c. "Two Aspects of Language and Two Types of Aphasic Disturbances." In Jakobson 1984. II:239–59.

——. 1960a. "Concluding Statement: Linguistics and Poetics." *Style in Language*. Ed. Thomas A. Sebeok. Cambridge, Mass.: MIT Press. 355–73.

——. 1960b. "Linguistics and Communication Theory." In Jakobson 1984. II: 570–79.

——. 1960c. "Parts and Wholes in Language." In Jakobson 1984. II:281–84.

——. 1963. "Toward a Linguistic Classification of Aphasic Impairment." In Jakobson 1984. II:287–306.

——. 1964. "Minutes of Study Group in Linguistics and Psychoanalysis." Mimeographed manuscript. The New Psychoanalytical Institute, New York.

——. 1965a. "Quest for the Essence of Language." *Diogenes* 51:21–37.

——. 1965b. "Vers une science de l'art poétique. *Théorie de la littérature: Textes des formalistes russes*. Ed. Tzvetan Todorov. Paris: Seuil. 9–13.

——. 1966. "Linguistic Types of Aphasia." In Jakobson 1984. II:307–33.

——. 1968. "Poetry of Grammar and Grammar of Poetry." In Jakobson 1984. III:87–97.

——. 1970. "Language in Relation to Other Communication Systems." In Linguaggi nella societiá nella tecnica, Milano (Ediziona de communítá).

——. 1975. *Coup d'oeuil sur le développement de la sémiotique*. Bloomington: Indiana Univ. Press: Studies in Securities v. 3.

——. 1976. "Petr Bogatyrev: Expert in Transfiguration." In Matejka, 29–39.

——. 1977. "A Few Remarks on Peirce, Pathfinder in the Science of Language." *Modern Language Notes* 92:1026–32.

——. 1980. *The Framework of Language*. Ann Arbor: Univ. of Michigan Press.

——. 1984. *Selected Writings*. Giravenhage: Mouton.

——. 1987. "On the Relation Between Visual and Auditority Signs." In *Language in Literature*. Ed. Krystyna Pomorska and Steven Rudy. Cambridge, Mass.: Belknap Press.

——. 1990. Langue and parole: Code and Meanings. In *On Language. Results of the Conference on Anthropology and Linguistics*. Ed. By Carl F. Voegelin and Thomas A. Sebeok. *International Journal of Linguistics. Memoir* 8:11–21.

Jakobson, Roman, and Petr Bogatyrev. 1929. "Die Folklore als eine besondere Art des Schaffens." *Donum natalicum Schrijnen*. Nijmegen-Utrecht. 900–913.

Jakobson, Roman, and Jurij Tynjanov. 1972. "Problems in the Study of Language and Literature." In *The Structuralists: From Marx to Lévi-Strauss*. Garden City, N.Y.: Anchor. 81–83.

Jakobson, Roman, and Linda R. Waugh. 1979. *The Sound Shape of Language*. Bloomington: Indiana Univ. Press.

Jameson, Fredric. 1984. Foreword. In Lyotard, vii–xxi.

——. 1991. *Postmodernism, or, The Cultural Logic of Late Capitalism*. Durham: Duke Univ. Press.

Keesing, M. Roger. 1987. "Anthropology as Interpretive Quest." *Current Anthropology* 28.2:161–76.

Kleinmann, Arthur. 1988. *Rethinking Psychiatry: From Cultural Category to Personal Experience.* New York: Free Press.

Klemenčič, Matjaž. 1995. *Slovenes in Cleveland. The Creation of a New Nation and a New World Community. Slovenia and the Slovenes of Cleveland, Ohio.* Novo Mesto: Dolenjska zalo ba.

Kluckhohn, Clyde. 1942. "Myths and Rituals: A General Theory." *Harvard Theological Review.* 35:45–79.

Kos, Milko. 1955. *Zgodovina slovencev ot naselitive do petnajstega stoletija.* Ljubljana: Slovenska Matica.

Kristeva, Julia. 1980. *Desire in Language: A Semiotic Approach to Language and Art.* New York: Columbia Univ. Press.

Kuhn, Thomas S. 1962. *The Structure of the Scientific Revolutions.* Chicago: Univ. of Chicago Press.

Kuper, Adam. 1988. *The Invention of Primitive Society: Transformations of an Illusion.* London and New York: Routledge.

Kutrzeba-Pojnarowa, Anna. 1983. "The Notion of Space and the Rural Exodus." In Portis-Winner and Susel, 67–82.

Lacan, Jacques. 1970–71. *Ecrits.* Paris: Seuil.

Lee, Benjamin. 1985. "Peirce, Frege, Saussure, and Whorf: The Semiotic Mediation of Ontology." In Mertz and Parmentier, 91–128.

Lévi-Strauss, Claude. 1963. *Structural Anthropology.* New York: Basic Books.

——. 1963–71. *Mythologiques.* 4 vols. Paris: Plon.

——. 1969. *The Raw and the Cooked.* New York: Harper & Row.

——. 1995. *Myth and Meaning.* New York: Schocken.

——. 1985. "Structuralism and Ecology." In *The View From Afar.* New York: Basic Books. 101–20.

Lewis, Oscar. 1951. *Life in a Mexican Village: Tepoztlán Restudied.* Urbana: Univ. of Illinois Press.

Lixačev, D. S. and A. M. Pančenko. 1984. *Smexovoj mir drevnej Rusi.* [The World of Laughter of Ancient Rus']. Leningrad: Nauka.

Ljubljanski regionalni zavod. 1985. *Ljubljanski regionalni zavod za varstvo naravne in kulturne dediščine za celotno območje občine Cerknica za potrebe prostorskih izvedbenih načrtov.* [Ljubljiana Regional Institute for the Protection of the Natural and Cultural Heritage for the Entire Area of the Cerknica District for the Use of Spatial of Planning]. Ljubljana: computer print-out.

Lord, Albert Bates. 1981. *The Singer of Tales.* Cambridge, Mass.: Harvard Univ. Press.

Lotman, Yury M. 1974a. "Observations on the Structure of the Narrative Text." *Soviet Studies in Literature* 10.4:75–81.

———. 1975a. "On the Metalanguage of a Typological Description of Culture." *Semiotica* 14.2:97–123.

———. 1975b. "Theater and Theatricality in the Order of Early Nineteenth-Century Culture." *Semiotics and Structuralism.* 155–85.

———. 1976a. *Semiotics of Cinema.* Ann Arbor: Department of Slavic Languages and Literature. Original publication in Russian, 1970.

———. 1976b. *Analysis of the Poetic Text.* Ann Arbor: Ardis.

———. 1977a. "The Dynamic Model of a Semiotic System." *Semiotica* 21.3/4:193–210.

———. 1977b. *The Structure of the Artistic Text.* Ann Arbor: Department of Slovic Languages and Literature. Original publication in Russian, 1970.

———. 1984. "The Poetics of Everyday Behavior in Russian Eighteenth-Century Culture." In Lotman and Uspensky 1984, 231–56.

———. 1990. *The Universe of the Mind: A Semiotic Theory of Culture.* Bloomington: Indiana Univ. Press.

———. 1992. *Kul'tura i vzryv.* Moscow: Gnosis.

———. 1994. "Text Within a Text." *PMLA* (May): 377–84.

Lotman, Yury, and A. M. Pjatigorsky. 1978. "Text and Function." *New Literary History* 9.2:233–44.

Lotman, Yury, and B. A. Uspensky. 1978. "On the Semiotic Mechanism of Culture." *New Literary History* 9:233–44.

———. 1984. *The Semiotics of Russian Culture.* Ann Arbor: Department of Slovic Languages and Literatures.

Lotman, Yury, L. A. Ginsburg. 1985. *The Semiotics of Russian Cultural History: Essays.* Ithaca: Cornell Univ. Press.

Luria, A. R. 1958. "Brain Disorders and Language Analysis." *Language and Speech* 1:14–34.

Lyotard, Jean-François. 1984. *The Postmodern Condition: A Report on Knowledge.* Minneapolis: Univ. of Minnesota Press.

Maddox, Richard Frederick. 1986. *Religion, Honor, and Patronage: A Study of Culture and Power in an Andalusian Town.* Ann Arbor: University Microfilms.

Maine, Henry Sumner, Sir. 1876. *Village-Communities in the East and West: Six Lectures Delivered at Oxford, to Which Are Added Other Lectures, Addresses and Essays.* London: John Murray.

Mal, J. 1928. *Zgodovina slovenskega naroda. Najnovejša doba* [The History of the Slovene People. The Modern Period]. Celje: Družba sv. Mohorja.

Manganaro, Marc, ed. 1990. *Modernist Anthropology: From Fieldwork to Text.* Princeton: Princeton Univ. Press.

Marcus, George E. 1986. "A Beginning." *Cultural Anthropology* 1.1:3–5.

———, ed. 1992. *Rereading Cultural Anthropology.* Durham: Duke Univ. Press.

———. 1993. *Perilous States: Conversations on Culture, Politics, and Nation.* Chicago: Univ. of Chicago Press.

Marcus, George E., and Michael M. J. Fischer. 1986. *Anthropology as Cultural Critique: An Experimental Moment in the Human Sciences.* Chicago: Univ. of Chicago Press.

Marcus, George E., and Richard Cushman. 1982. "Ethnographies as Text." *Annual Review of Anthropology* 11:25–69.

Margolis, Joseph. 1991. *The Truth about Relativism.* Cambridge, Mass.: Blackwell.

———. 1993. "Texts." *Poetics Today* 14.1: 193–211.

———. 1999. Selves and Other Texts." *Annual ICPQ Proceedings.* 1–29.

Matejka, Ladislav, ed. 1976. *Sound, Sign, and Meaning: Quinquagenery of the Prague Linguistic Circle.* Ann Arbor: Department of Slavic Languages and Literatures.

Matejka, Ladislav, and Irwin R. Titunik, eds. 1976. *Semiotics of Art: Prague School Contributions.* Cambridge, Mass.: MIT Press.

McGowan, John. 1991. *Postmodernism and Its Critics.* Ithaca: Cornell Univ. Press.

McKenzie, D. F. 1999. *Bibliography and the Sociology of Texts.* Cambridge: Cambridge Univ. Press.

Melik, Anton. 1963. *Slovenija: geografski opis.* Vol. 1. Ljubljana: Slovenska matica.

Mead, Margaret. 1976. "Toward a Human Science." *Science* 191/4230: 90.

Mertz, Elizabeth and Richard J. Parmentier, eds. 1985. *Semiotic Mediation: Sociocultural and Psychological Perspectives.* Orlando: Academic Press.

Milun, Kathryn. 1993. "Returning to Eastern Europe." In Marcus 1993, 53–79.

Minnich, Robert Gary. 1979. *The Homemade World of Zagaj: An Interpretation of the "Practical Life" among Traditional Peasant-Farmers in West Haloze— Slovenia, Yugoslavia.* Bergen: Sosialantropologisk Institutt Universitetet Bergen.

———. 1993. "Reflections on a Violent Death of a Multi-Ethnic State: A Slovene Perspective." *Anthropology of East Europe Review* 11.182:77–84.

Molek, Ivan. 1978. *Two Worlds.* Dover, Del.: M. Molek.

——. 1979. *Slovene Immigrant History, 1900–1950: Autobiographical Sketches.* Dover, Del.: M. Molek.

Molek, Mary. 1976. *Immigrant Woman.* Dover, Del.: M. Molek.

Morson, Gary Saul. 1978. "The Heresiarch of *Meta.*" PTL 3.3:407–27.

Morson, Gary Saul, and Caryl Emerson. 1990. *Mikhail Bakhtin: Creation of a Prosaics.* Stanford: Stanford Univ. Press.

——, eds. 1989. *Rethinking Bakhtin: Extensions and Challenges.* Evanston, Ill.: Northwestern Univ. Press.

Moseley, Phillip E. 1940. "The Peasant Family: The *zadruga* or Communal Joint-Family in the Balkans and Its Recent Evolution." In *The Cultural Approach to History.* Ed. Caroline F. Marc. New York: Columbia Univ. Press

——. 1953. "The Distribution of the *zadruga* within Southeastern Europe." In *The Joshua Starr Memorial Volume: Studies in History and Philology.* New York: Conference on Jewish Relations.

Mukařovský, Jan. 1934. "Art As a Semiotic Fact." In Mukařovský 1978, 82–88.

——. 1935. Replika J. Mukařovského. *Slovo a slovesnost* 1 (1935): 190–93.

——. 1936. *Aesthetic Function, Norm and Value as Social Facts.* Ann Arbor: Department of Slavic Languages and Literatures.

——. 1937. "The Aesthetic Norm." In Mukařovský 1978, 49–56.

——. 1944. "The Essence of the Visual Arts." In Mukařovský, 1978. 220–35.

——. 1978. *Structure, Sign and Function. Selected Essays by Jan Mukařovský.* New Haven: Yale Univ. Press.

——. 1982. "Structuralism in Aesthetics and in Literary Studies." In Steiner, 65–82.

Nöth, Winfried. 1990. *Handbook of Semiotics.* Bloomington: Indiana Univ. Press.

O'Neill, Theresa D. 1994. "Telling about Whites, Talking about Indians: Oppression, Resistance, and Contemporary American Indian Identity." *Cultural Anthropology* 9.1: 94–126.

Opler, Morris, and R. D. Singh. 1948. "The Division of Labor in an Indian Village." In *A Reader in General Anthropology.* Ed. Carleton Stevens Coon. New York: Henry Holt. 464–69.

Parecles, Américo. 1993. *Folklore and Culture on the Texas-Mexican Border.* Austin: CMS Books.

Parmentier, Richard J. 1985a. "Semiotic Mediation: Ancestral Genealogy and Final Interpretant." In Mertz and Parmentier, 359–85.

——. 1985b. "The Sign's Place in medias res: Peirce's Concept of Semiotic Mediation." In Mertz and Parmentier, 23–48.

——. 1985c. "Times of the Signs: Modalities of History and Levels of Social Structure in Belau." In Mertz and Parmentier, 131–54.

——. 1987. *The Sacred Remains: Myth, History, and Polity in Belau.* Chicago: Univ. of Chicago Press.

Peacock, James. 1981. "The Third Stream: Weber, Parsons and Geertz." *Journal of the Anthropological Society of Oxford* 7:122–29.

Peirce, Charles Sanders. 1931–58. *Collected Papers.* 8 vols. Cambridge, Mass.: Harvard Univ. Press.

Peklaj, Andreja, Matja Kmecl, Peter Škoberne. 1994. *Cerkniško jezero.* Ljubljana: Narodna in univerzitetna knižnica.

Peklaj, Andreja, Kmecl, Matjaž, and Škoberne, Peter. 1994. *Cerkniško jezero.* UNESCO Publication.

Pelc, Jerzy. 1971. "On the Concept of Narration." *Semiotica* 31: 1–21.

Pjatigorsky, A. 1962. Nekotorye obščie zamečanija otnositel'no rassmotrenija teksta kak raznovidmost zmaka AN SSSR. Institut slavjanovedenija.

Pluto Pregelj, Leopoldina, and Carole Roget. 1996. *Historical Dictionary of Slovenia.* Lanham, Md.: Scarecrow Press.

Ponzio, Augusto. 1995. "The Symbol, Alterity, and Abduction." *Semiotica* 56. 34:261–77.

Portis-Winner, Irene. 1971. *A Slovenian Village: Žerovnica.* Providence, R.I.: Brown Univ. Press.

——. 1974. "The Peasant and the City. An Historical Perspective." Paper presented at International Symposium held at Brown University, Providence 197. Limited Distribution.

——. 1977a. "The Question of the *zadruga* in Slovenia: Myth and Reality in Žerovnica." *Anthropological Quarterly* 50: 125–34.

——. 1977b. "The Semiotic Character of the Aesthetic Function as Defined by the Prague Linguistic Circle." In *Language and Thought: Anthropological Issues.* Ed. William C. McCormack and Stephen A. Wurm. The Hague: Mouton. 407–40.

——. 1978a. "Cultural Semiotics and Anthropology." In Bailey, Matejka, and Steiner, 335–63.

——. 1978b. "Ethnicity among Urban Slovene Villagers in Cleveland, Ohio." *Papers in Slovene Studies* (1977): 61–63.

——. 1978d. "The Question of the Cultural Point of View in Determining Boundaries of Ethnic Units." *Papers in Slovene Studies* (1997): 73–82.

——. 1983a. "Ethnicity and Communication." *Slovene Studies* 3:119–26.

——. 1983b. "Some Comments on the Concept of the Human Sign. Visual and

Verbal Components and Applications to Ethnic Research: A Wonderful Father." In Herzfeld, 213–285.

——. 1984a. "Lotman and Semiotics of Culture." *Semiosis, Semiotics and the History of Culture: In honorem Georgii Lotman.* Ed. Morris Halle. Ann Arbor: Univ. of Michigan Press.

——. 1984b. "Theories of Narration and Ethnic Culture Texts." In *Sign, System, and Function: Papers of the First and Second Polish-American Semiotics Colloquia.* Ed. Jerzy Pelc et al. Berlin and New York: Mouton. 439–55.

——. 1987a. "Cultural Semiotics versus Other Cultural Sciences." In *A Plea for Cultural Semiotics.* Ed. Achim Eschbach and Walter A. Koch. Bochum: N. Brockmeyer. 4–22.

——. 1987b. "Metonymic Metaphors and Ethnicity: Slovenes in Cleveland." In M. S. Priestly, O. B. Nedeljkovic and H. R. Cooper, Jr. *Ljubi Slovenci. A Festschrift for Rado L. Lenček. Slovene Studies.* 9/1–2. Pp. 243–51.

——. 1988a. "Ethnic Culture Texts as Narration." In *Literary Anthropology: A New Interdisciplinary Approach to People, Signs, and Literature.* Amsterdam and Philadelphia: J. Benjamins. 127–40.

——. 1988b. "Report on Research in the Semiotics of Culture." *The Semiotic Web* (1987): 601–36.

——. 1989a. "Culture and Semiotics: Perspectives for the Future of a Potential Discipline." In *Culture and Semiotics.* Ed. Walter A. Koch. Bochum: N. Brockmeyer.

——. 1989b. "The Human Sign as an Integrative Concept in the Semiotics of Culture." In *The Nature of Culture: Proceedings of the International and Interdisciplinary Symposium,* Oct. 7–11, 1986. Ed. Walter A. Koch. Bochum: Studienverlag Brockmeyer. 369–87.

——. 1989c. "Segmentation and Reconstruction of Ethnic Culture Texts and the Interpenetration of Verbal and Visual Spheres." In *Issues in Slavic Literary and Cultural Theory.* Ed. Karl Eimermacher, Peter Grzybek, and Georg Witte. Bochum: N. Brockmeyer. 411–31.

——. 1990a. "Anthropology and Semiotics." In *Semiotics in the Individual Sciences.* Ed. Walter A. Koch. Bochum: N. Brockmeyer. 619–48.

——. 1990b. "How Ethnic Texts Speak." In *Semiotics and the Arts: Festschrift for Thomas G. Winner.* Ed. L. Mandelker, R. Matejka, and E. Stankiewicz. San Diego: Charles Schlacks. 173–87.

——. 1992. "Transnationals and the Human Sign: Modes of Signification." In *Kultur, Evolution: Fallstudien und Synthese.* Ed. Marlene Landsch, Heiko Karnowski, and Ivan Bystřina. Frankfurt/Main: Peter Lang.

——. 1994c. *Semiotics of Culture: The "Strange Intruder."* Bochum: N. Brockmeyer.

——. 1994a. "Peirce, Saussure and Jakobson's Aesthetic Function." Ed. Herman Parret. Amsterdam: John Benjamins.

——. 1996. "Jakobson's World; His Dialog with Peirce. Implication on American Anthropology." In M. Mikulášek and Danuše Kšicová, eds. *Litteraria humanitas.* IV. Brno: Masaryk University Press.

——. 1998. "Bakhtin and Contemporary Anthropology." *Elementa Journal of Slavic Studies and Comparative Cultural Semiotics.* Special Issue on M. M. Bakhtin 4.1:17–44.

Portis-Winner, Irene, and Thomas G. Winner. 1976. "The Semiotics of Culture Texts." *Semiotica* 18.2:101–156.

Portis-Winner, Irene, and Jean Umiker-Sebeok, eds. 1979. *Semiotics of Culture.* The Hague: Mouton.

Portis-Winner, Irene, and Rudolph M. Susel, eds. 1983. *The Dynamics of East European Ethnicity Outside of Eastern Europe: With Special Emphasis on the American Case.* Cambridge, Mass.: Schenkman.

Portis-Winner, Irene, and Thomas G. Winner, eds. 1984. *The Peasant and the City in Eastern Europe: Interpenetrating Structures.* Cambridge, Mass.: Schenkman.

Putnam, Hilary. 1992. *Renewing Philosophy.* Cambridge, Mass.: Harvard Univ. Press.

Rabinow, Paul. 1986. "Representations Are Social Facts: Modernity and Post-Modernity." In Clifford and Marcus, 234–61.

——. 1988. "Beyond Ethnography: Anthropology as Nominalism." *Cultural Anthropology* 34:355–61.

Rabinow, Paul and William M. Sullivan, eds. 1979. *Interpretive Social Science: A Reader.* Berkeley and Los Angeles: Univ. of California Press.

Ramovš, Franc. 1931. *Dialektološka karta slovenskega jezika* Ljubljana: Universitetna tiskarna.

——. 1936. *Kratka zgodovina slovenskega jezika* Ljubljana: Akademska zaloč ba.

——. 1957. *Karta slovenskih narečij v priročni izdaji* Ljubljana: Cankarjeva zalo ba.

Rasmussen, D. and M. 1971. *Mythic Symbolic Language and Philosophical Anthropology: A Constructive Interpretation of the Thought of Paul Ricoeur.* The Hague: Nijhoff.

Redfield, Robert. 1930. *Tepoztlán, a Mexican Village: A Study of the Folk Life.* Chicago: Univ. of Chicago Press.

Ricoeur, Paul. 1971a. "The Model of the Text: Meaningful Action Considered As a Text." *Social Research* 38:529–62.

Riesman, David. 1950. *The Lonely Crowd: A Study of the Changing American Character.* New Haven: Yale Univ. Press.

Robbe-Grillet, Alain. 1988. "The French Novel: From the *nouveau* to the New." *Times Literary Supplement* Oct. 13–19, 1988: 1122–23.

Rosaldo, Renato, 1986. "Llongot Hunting as Story and Experience." In Turner, 97–138.

——. 1995. "Bridging Diversity." *Anthropological Newsletter* 36.5:9.

Runes, Dagobert D. 1942. *The Dictionary of Philosophy.* New York: Philosophical Library.

Saussure, Ferdinand de. 1966. *Course in General Linguistics.* New York: McGraw Hill.

Šabec, Nada. 1995. *Half pa pu: The Language of Slovene Americans.* Ljubljana: Škuc.

Savan, David. 1987–88. *An Introduction to C. S. Peirce's Full System of Semeiotic.* Toronto: Toronto Semiotic Circle.

Schechner, Richard. 1985. *Between Theater and Anthropology.* Philadelphia: Univ. of Pennsylvania Press.

Scheffler, Israel. 1974. *Four Pragmatists: A Critical Introduction to Peirce, James, Mead, and Dewey.* London: Routledge & Kegan Paul.

Segre, Cesare. 1979. *Structures and Time: Narration, Poetry, Models.* Chicago: Univ. of Chicago Press.

Shakespeare, William. 1943. "Measure for Measure." *The Comedies of Shakespeare.* v.1: 203–39. New York: The Modern Library.

Shankman, Paul. 1984. "The Thick and the Thin: On the Interpretive Theoretical Program of Clifford Geertz." *Current Anthropology* 25.3: 261–79.

Shattuck, Roger. 1996. *Forbidden Knowledge: From Prometheus to Pornography.* New York: St. Martin's Press.

Sheriff, John K. 1994. *Charles Peirce's Guess at the Riddle: Grounds for Human Significance.* Bloomington: Indiana Univ. Press.

Silverstein, Michael. 1987. Foreword. Parmentier, xi–xvi.

Singer, Milton B. 1984. *Man's Glassy Essence: Explorations in Semiotic Anthropology.* Bloomington: Indiana Univ. Press.

Stallybras, Peter. 1985. " 'Drunk with the Cup of Liberty': Robin Hood, the Carnivalesque and the Rhetoric of Violence in Early Modern England." *Semiotica* 54.1–2: 113–45.

Stankiewicz, Edward. 1991. "The Concept of Structure in Contemporary Linguistics." In *Current Issues in Linguistic Theory.* Ed. L. Waugh and S. Rudy. vol. 49: 11–32. Amsterdam: John Benjamins.

Steiner, Peter, ed. 1982. *The Prague School: Selected Writings, 1929–1946.* Austin: Univ. of Texas Press.

Strathern, Marilyn. 1987. "Intervening." Review essay on *Waiting: The Whites of South Africa* by Vincent Crapanzano. *Cultural Anthropology* 2.2:255–87.

Susel, Rudolph M. 1993. "The Perpetuation and Transformation of Ethnic Identity among Slovene Immigrants in America and the American-Born Generations: Continuity and Change." In Portis-Winner and Susel, 109–32.

Tambiah, Stanley. 1988. "Ethnic Conflict in the World Today." *American Ethnologist* 16.2:335–49.

Tamir, Yael. 1993. *Liberal Nationalism.* Princeton: Princeton Univ. Press.

Tarn, Nathaniel. 1991. *Views from the Weaving Mountain: Selected Essays in Poetics Anthropology.* Albuquerque: Univ. of New Mexico Press.

Tedlock, Dennis, and Bruce Mannheim, eds. 1995. *The Dialogic Emergence of Culture.* Urbana: Univ. of Illinois Press.

Thompson, John B. 1984. *Studies in the Theory of Ideology.* Berkeley: Univ. of California Press.

Todorov, Tzvetan. 1978. "The Birth of Occidental Semiotics." In Bailey and Steiner, 1–42.

——. 1984. Mikhail Bakhtin: *The Dialogical Principle.* Minneapolis: Univ. of Minnesota Press.

Tomasevich, Jožo. 1955. *Peasant Politics and Economic Change in Yugoslavia.* Stanford: Stanford Univ. Press.

Tomasić, Dinko. 1948. *Personality and Culture in Eastern European Politics.* New York: G. W. Stewart.

Tončić, Dragutin. 1902. *Zakon od 9. svibnja 1889 o zadrugama i zakon od 30. travnja 1902 o promjeni odnosno nadopunjenju nekih ustanova zak. od 9. svibnja 1889 o zadrugama.* Zagreb.

Toynbee, Arnold Joseph. 1934. *A Study of History.* London: Oxford Univ. Press.

Turner, Victor. 1964. "Betwixt and Between: The Liminal Period in *rites de passage.*" *Symposium on New Approaches to the Study of Religion: Proceedings of the 1964 Annual Spring Meeting of the American Ethnological Society.* Ed. June Helm. 4–20.

——. 1970. *The Forest of Symbols: Aspects of Nolembu Ritual.* Ithaca: Cornell Univ. Press.

——. 1982. "From Ritual to Theater." *American Performing Arts Journal.*

——. 1984. "Liminality and the Performance Genre." In *Rite, Drama, Festival, Rehearsal: Toward a Theory of Performance.* Ed. John Jay McAloon. Philadelphia: Ishi.

——. 1986. *The Anthropology of Performance.* New York: PAJ Publications.

Tyler, Stephen A. 1986a. "Introduction to Cultural Anthropology." *Cultural Anthropology* 1.2:131–37.

——. 1986b. "Post-Modern Ethnography: From Document of the Occult to Occult Document." In Clifford and Marcus, 122–40.

——. 1987. *The Unspeakable: Discourse, Dialogue, and Rhetoric in the Postmodern World.* Madison: Univ. of Wisconsin Press.

Urban, G. 1985. "The Semiotics of Two Speech Styles in Shokleng." In Mertz and Parmentier, 311–57.

Uspensky, Boris A. n.d. "History and Semiotics: The Perception of Time as A Semiotic Problem." Unpublished translation from the Russian original.

Valvasor, Johann W. 1689. *Die Ehre des Erzherzogtums Crain* Ljubljana. 4 vols.

Vatimo, Gianni. 1985. *La fine della modernitá: nihilismo ed ermeneutica nella cultura post-moderna.* Rome: Garzanti.

Vernadsky, V. I. 1960. *Izbrannye sochinenija.* Vol. 5. Moscow.

——. 1988. Razmyšlenija naturalista. Naučnaja mysl' kak planetarnoe javlenie. Book 2. Moscow.

Vico, Giovanni. 1835–7. *Principi di una sciencia nuova.* Milano.

Vilfan, Sergij. 1961. *Pravna zgodovina Slovencev; ot naselitve do zloma stare Jugoslavije.* Ljubljana: Slovenska Matica.

Voloshinov, V. N. 1973. *Marxism and the Philosophy of Language.* New York: Seminar Press.

Vygotsky, L. S. 1965. *Thought and Language.* Cambridge, Mass.: MIT Press.

——. 1971. *The Psychology of Art.* Cambridge, Mass.: MIT Press.

Ware, Caroline F., ed. *The Cultural Approach to History.* New York: Columbia Univ. Press.

Wertsch, James B. 1985. "The Semiotic Mediation of Mental Life: L. S. Vygotsky and M. M. Bakhtin." In Mertz and Parmentier, 49–70.

White, Allan. 1985. "Hysteria and the End of the Carnival: Festivity and Bourgeois Neurosis." *Semiotics* 54.1–2: 97–111.

Winner, Thomas G. 1984. "Roman Jakobson's Poetics: On the Occasion of Volume III of Roman Jakobson's *Selected Writings.*" Review. *International Journal of Slavic Linguistics and Poetics* v.30: 159–71.

Wolf, Eric R. 1962. "Cultural Dissonance in the Italian Alps." *Comparative Studies in Society and History* 5:1–14.

———. 1966. *Peasants.* Englewood Cliffs, N.J.: Prentice-Hall.

———. 1982. *Europe and the People without History.* Los Angeles and Berkeley: Univ. of California Press.

———. 1988. "Inventing Society." *American Ethnologist* 15(4): 752–61.

———. 1999. *Envisioning Power: Ideologies of Dominance and Crisis.* Berkeley and Los Angeles: Univ. of California Press.

Yates, Frances A. 1966. *The Art of Memory.* Chicago: Univ. of Chicago Press.

Index

Page numbers appearing in italics refer to illustrations.

Abduction, 71, 72, 155
Acculturation, 21
Adorno, Theodor W., , 68
Agrarian crisis (1890s), 88
Albanians, Islamic conversion of, 19
Alexander I, king of the Serbs, Croats, and Slovenes, 90
Alpine inns, 137
American Slovene Catholic Union (Ameriška Slovenska Katoliška Jednota; Cleveland), 109
Ameriška domovina (American Homeland), 111
Ameriški Slovenec (The American Slovene), 111
Anderson, Benedict, 37–38
Anthropology: dialogic, 50, 64–66, 153; interpretative, 43–45; performance, 43, 45–46
Aristophanes, 85–86
Artifice, 55, 104–5, 158n.3
Artistic texts, 57
Ashley, David, 68
Astructural vs. structural, 56
Augustine, Saint, 5–6
Austerlitz, battle of (1812), 39
Austrian decrees (1848 and 1849), 87
Authorial voice, 44
Authoritative voice of the ethnographer, 130
Autobiographies of Slovene villagers, 98–103

Bahloul, Joëlle, 46, 47–49, 154
Bakhtin, Mikhail, 154; and Bahloul, 48; on carnival reversals in hierarchies, 47, 60, 65, 66; dialogic program of, 50, 64–66, 153; on double voicing, 67, 70, 118; on ethnicity, 131; on heteroglossia, 50, 153; influence of, 6, 158 n.1; on language under communism, 64; on laughter, 60, 65; on novelization, 64;

on official ideology vs. indigenous life/traditions/values, 36; on official vs. nonofficial culture, 72; and Turner, 45
Balina (game), 13, 15, 66, 157 n.1
Barth, Frederick, 8
Barthes, Roland, 50, 131
Baudelaire, Charles, 33
Baudrillard, Jean, 68
Belau (Caroline Islands), 61
Binary index, 45
Biosphere, 63
Bloke (mountain range), 78, 79
Boas, Franz, 33
Bogatyrev, Petr, 6; on folk costumes, 53–54, 131; Jakobson on, 52; on multiple identities, 32
Boissevain, Jeremy, 35–36, 38–40
Bosnians, Islamic conversion of, 19
Bosnian war, 94
Boundaries, 50, 59–60, 135–36
Bourdieu, Pierre, 67–68, 73
Brest furniture factory: Martinjak, Slovenia, 11, 17; Žerovnica, Slovenia, 20, 90–91
Bricoleur, 137
Brockway settlement (Minnesota), 123
Bühler, Karl, 53, 54
Button box music, 66

Calumet settlement (Michigan), 123
Carinthian dialect *(notranjski dialekt),* 77
Carniola (Kranj; Slovenia), 107
Carniolan Slovenian Catholic Society (Kranjsko–Slovenska Katoliška Jednota; Cleveland), 109
Cassirer, Ernst, 158 n.2
Caton, Steven C., 55
Cattle trading, 87
Celebrations, revitalization of, 38–40
Ceremony. *See* Tradition
Cerknica basin (Cerkniško polje), 78, 79
Cerknica Lake (Cerkniško jezero; pre-

Cerknica Lake (*continued*)
sihajoče; Žerovnica, Slovenia), 11, 14,
157 n.2; draining/flooding of, 78, 79–
80, 138; electric pumping model of, 39,
59, 97–98; fishing in, 80; geological
foundation of, 78; land use at, 78–79;
myths/folk tales about, 79, 81–83; origin of, 81–83; sink holes of *(požiral-
nike)*, 78, 158 n.1; as tourist attraction,
59, 95–96, 97–98, 103–4; writings on,
79
Cevc, Tone: *The Slovene Hayrack,* 59
Chance/determinacy, 62
Cleveland Ethnic Heritage Studies Development Program, 23
Cleveland settlement, 20–27, 106–24; arts
in, 110–11; businesses/organizations
of, 23, *24,* 109–12; carnival behavior in,
66; Catholic church in, 109–10; Catholic vs. secular, socialist immigrants,
21, 112; cooperative programs of, 23,
109; economic success in, 117; elders in,
support of, 127–29, 153; establishment
of, 3; food/supplies sent to Europe by
immigrants in, 22; friendliness/hospi-
tality of, 23; houses in, 23, 127–28;
identity in, 26; immigration and settlement history, 106–12; inner-city
blight in, 26–27; inner story of early
experiences in, 112–23; internal vs. external space of, 59–60; and kin back
home, 112, 152–53; method of studying, 21, 23, 25, 27; music in, 113, 114,
116–17; national homes in, 23, 26–27,
110, 152–53; newspapers in, 111; objects
as symbols in, 61, 115; poverty in, 113–
14, 115; St. Clair Avenue, 23, *24,* 26–27,
128; St. Lawrence, 25–26, 109, 111; St.
Vitus, 23, 26–27, 109, 111; saloons in,
110; size of, 107; Slovene/English used
in, 108, 111; traditions as reemerging/
retained in, 39, 112–13; upward mobility in, 25–26; upward mobility of
youth in, 152; work ethic in, 106, 148–
49; written documents of, 117–23;
Žerovnica connections, evidence of, 5
Clevelandska Amerika (Cleveland America*),* 111, 112
Cominform, 92

Communication, 46
Communism, European collapse of, 18
Conceptual thinking, 45
Connerton, Paul, 46–47
Cooperative programs, 23, 109
Čop, J.: *The Slovene Hayrack,* 59
Costumes, 53–54, 131
Course in General Linguistics (Saussure),
6–7
Crapanzano, Vincent, 44, 69, 70, 153
Croats, Catholicism of, 19
Cultural explosion, 153
Culture texts, 7, 43, 44, 56–59, 72–73, 153
Custom. *See* Tradition

Dalton, John, 72
Daniel, E. Valentine, 157–58 n.1
Dar-Refayil household (Setij, Algeria),
47–49, 154
Debevc, Anton ("Tone"), and family,
136–42, 152
Debevc, Ivan, 140
Depression years (1920s and 1930s), 88–
89
Derrida, Jacques, 72
Determinacy/chance, 62
De Vos, George A., 33–34
Dialogic anthropology, 50, 64–66, 153
Discipline, 148, 149, 150
Docherty, Thomas, 68
Dolenjski (Slovenia), 107
Domobranci (Slovene fighters or par-
tisans), 44
Double consciousness, 118
Doublespeak, 72
Double voicing, 67, 70, 118
Dreams, perception in, 61–62
Dreyfus, Hubert, 67–68

East vs. West, 40–41
Eco, Umberto, 73
Eisenstein, Sergei: *The Strike,* 57
Enlightenment, 41–42, 67, 68
Ethnicity, 33–35; and authoritative voice
of the ethnographer, 130; dynamics of,
41–42, 131; exploitation of, 41–42
Ethnic network map, 121, 122
Ethnic violence, 8, 9, 18, 38
Evans-Pritchard, E. E., 85
Everyday behavior, 50, 60, 154

Fact vs. theory, 71–72
Fél, Edit, 40–41
Feudal period, 80–81
Fieldwork, 130–31
Firstness/Secondness/Thirdness, 50, 52, 54–55, 70, 153, 155, 158 n.2
Fischer, Michael M. J., 34
Forest land, 87, *135*
Foucault, Michel, 33, 68
Franz-Joseph (emperor of Austro-Hungary), 111
Freud, Sigmund, 68

Geertz, Clifford, 4, 44, 45, 56
Generosity/hospitality, 148, 150–51
Gesture, 53
Glas naroda (The Voice of the People, NYC), 111
Glasnost, 18
Glazer, Nathan, 33
Globalization, 3
Godeša, Andreja, 98–100
Goodman, Nelson, 72
Gorbachev, Mikhail, 18
Gospodar/gospodinja (head of family or household), 26, 157 n.6
Grabelšek, Julia, 140, 141–42
Grdina family, 23, 143, 150
Greek myths, 85–86
Guthrie, W. K. C., 85–86

Habits, 47, 51
Hace, M.: *The Smugglers,* 87
Halbwachs, Maurice, 46
Hammel, Eugene, 9, 41, 69
Hayden, Robert, 9, 37
Hermeneutics of suspicion, 68
Herzegovinians, Islamic conversion of, 19
Herzfeld, Michael, 40, 46, 49, 155
Heteroglossia, 50, 153
Hibbing settlement (Minnesota): establishment of, 3; method of studying, 23, 25, 27; objects as symbols in, 61; traditions as reemerging in, 39
History and memory, 45–49; semiotics of, 50, 61–62, 70; and viability of memories, 85
Hobsbawm, Eric, 35–36, 37–38
Hody (a pig slaughtering feast), 40

Hofer, Tamás, 34, 35–36, 40–41, 130, 154
Holton, Gerald, 69, 71–72
Horse smuggling, 87, 131–32
Hospitality/generosity, 148, 150–51
Human sign. *See* Man-sign
Human signs in cultural context: Debevc family as, 136–42, 152; Jakšič family as, 143–51, 152; Rok family as, 133–36, *135,* 152
Humor, 66
Hungarian folk art, 40–41

Ibsen, Henrik, 123
Icon/Index/Symbol, 50, 51, 52, 55, 61, 70, 153, 158 n.2
Imagined communities, 35–38
Immediate/Dynamic/Final Interpretant, 50, 158 n.3
Immigrants. *See* Cleveland settlement; Hibbing settlement
Immigrant Woman (M. Molek), 117–21, 123, 152
Individuals, 31–32
Inner point of view, 43–49
Insurance agencies, 109, 112
Interpretative anthropology, 43–45
Ivan Cankar Dramatic Society (Cleveland), 110, 117
Ivanov, V. V., 6, 56

Jakobson, Roman, 6; on artifice, 55, 104–5, 158 n.3; on dialogue, 64; influence of, 55, 157 n.1; on the man-sign, 52–53; on metonymic metaphors, 50, 54, 55; on Peirce, 52, 55, 158 n.3; in Prague Linguistic Circle, 7; on semiotics of culture, 50, 53, 54–55; on theory/fact, 71
Jakšič, Anna, and family, 73, 143–51, 152
Jameson, Fredric, 68
Janez (Slovene-American), 114–16
Javornik mountain range, 78, 97–98
Jenc, Tomaž, 101–2
Jews, French and Algerian, 47–49, 154
Joseph II, emperor of Germany, 81

Kant, Immanuel, 5–6
Kebe, Viktor, 98
Kleinman, Arthur, 128, 129
Kos, Milko, 86–87
Kosovo, 94

Kosovo polje (Ravens' Field), battle of (1389), 19
Kozolec (wooden hay rack), 58–59, 61, 115, *116*, 141
Križna gora (Mountain of the Crosses), 79, 97–98

Lacan, Jacques, 31
Language, 64, 68. *See also* Slovene language
Laughter, 60, 65–66
Law for the Protection of National Monuments (1981), 97
Legisign, 55, 153, 158n.2
Lévi-Strauss, Claude, 56, 69–70
Liminality, 45–46, 65–66
Linguistics vs. poetics, 53
Ljubljana (Slovenia), 81
Ljubljana–Trieste railway line, 87
Locke, John, 5–6
Logar family, 96, 97
Lotman, Yury, 6; on boundaries, 50, 59; on chance/determinacy, 62; on communication, 46; on cultural explosion, 153; on culture text, 43, 57; on ethnicity, 131; on everyday behavior, 50, 60, 154; on implicit/explicit montage, 50, 57–58, 66, 121; on internal transfiguration, 72; on laughter, 65–66; and the Moscow-Tartu School, 7; on multiple identities, 32; on pre-Christian practices in Russia, 47; semiosphere concept of, 63; on the Symbol, 61
Lower Carinthian dialect, 77
Lož valley, 78, 87
Lumber, 87
Lunka, Marija, 26, 27, 135–36. *See also* Rok, Matija: family of

Maine, Sir Henry Sumner, 86
Mannheim, Bruce, 64
Manning, R. F., 38
Man-sign, 5, 50, 52–53, 63
Marcus, George E., 69
Margolis, Joseph, 56, 69
Maria Theresa, Holy Roman Empress, 81
Marija (Slovene American), 113–14
Marof cooperative farm, 11, 16–17, 79–80, 90–91
Marx, Karl, 68

Mary (companion of Anna Jakšič), 143, 144, 146, 151, 152
Mehadžič, Vida, 100–101
Melik, Anton, 86–87
Melting pot, 130
Memory. *See* History and memory
Mendel, Gregor Johann, 72
Menisija mountain range, 78
Mertelj, Marija ("Micka"), 93
Minnich, Robert Gary, 9–10, 40
Modernism. *See* Postmodernism/modernism
Modernization, 93, 95, 127, 128–29
Molek, Ivan, 117; *Slovene Immigrant History, 1900–1950,* 118, 121–23, 152; *Two Worlds,* 118, 121
Molek, Mary: *Immigrant Woman,* 117–21, 123, 152
Montage: implicit/explicit, 50, 57–58, 66, 121, 131–32, 138–40, 151
Monument Protection Agency, 97
Moravia, 39–40
Moscow-Tartu School, 7, 44; on culture texts, 56–59; on everyday behavior, 60; influence of, 158 n.1; on semiotics of culture, 55, 56–63; on the structural vs. astructural, 56
Mosely, Phillip E., 84, 86–87
Moynihan, Daniel Patrick, 33
Mukařovský, Jan, 6, 7, 54, 104–5
Multiculturalism, 21, 130
Music in Cleveland settlement, 113, 114, 116–17
Mutual aid societies, 109
Myth and history, 69–70

Napoleon Bonaparte, 81
Napoleonic Illyria, 81
Narodna beseda (The National Word; Cleveland), 111
Nation, 31–33, 37, 40–41
National homes, 23, 26–27, 110, 152–53
Ndembu initiation rites, 45, 57, 65–66
Newton, Isaac, 72
Nietzsche, Friedrich, 68
Nostalgia, 153–55
Notranjski Regional Park (Slovenia), 98
Notranjsko (Slovenia), 107
Novelization, 64

Opler, Morris, 86
Otok (Slovenia), 97

Parmentier, Richard J., 55, 61, 62, 73
Patriarchal authority/discipline, 148, 149, 150
Peirce, Charles Sanders, 5; on abduction, 71, 155; on the binary index and conceptual thinking, 45; on communication, 46, 55; on double consciousness, 118; Eco on, 73; on experience, 71, 131; on Firstness/Secondness/Thirdness, 50, 52, 54–55, 70, 153, 155, 158 n.2; on the human sign, 50, 52–53, 63; on Icon/Index/Symbol, 50, 51, 52, 55, 61, 70, 153, 158 n.2; on Immediate/Dynamic/Final Interpretant, 50, 158 n.3; on infinite regress, 64; influence of, 54–55, 157–58 n.1; Legisign of, 55, 153, 158 n.2; on self as other, 32; on semiotics of culture, 51–53; sign as defined by, 6, 51
Pelc, Jerzy, 132
Pensions, 140–41
Perestroika, 18
Performance anthropology, 43, 45–46
Personality, semiotics of (semiosphere), 7, 63
Pjatigorsky, A., 56
Pluralism, 130
Poetics vs. linguistics, 53
Polovič, Meta, 93, 103
Popper, Karl, 71
Postmodernism/modernism, 32–33, 42, 50, 67–70
Postojna (Slovenia), 159 n.9
Poverty, 87, 88, 113–14, 115
Power, 62, 72–73
Prague Linguistic Circle (Prague School), 7, 53, 54, 61
Primožič, Tone, 26–27, 93, 94–95, 134–35, *135. See also* Rok, Matija: family of
Putnam, Hillary, 72

Rabinow, Paul, 32–33, 42, 67–68
Rakek (Slovenia), 87
Rakov Škocjan (Slovenia), 98
Ramovš, Franc, 77
Ranger, Terence, 35–36, 37–38
Representation, modern crisis of, 8–10

Rethemnos (Crete), 49
Revitalization of tradition, 38–40, 42
Ricoeur, Paul, 56, 68
Rok, Marija, 93. *See also* Rok, Matija: family of
Rok, Matija, *85;* courage/humor of, 134, 147; family of, 26, 27, 93, 133–36, *135,* 152; as village historian, 48, 84, 133, 134
Rorty, Richard, 72
Rosaldo, Renato, 35
Rot, Milan, 98
Rovtarski dialect, 77
Russian nobility: role playing by, 60

St. Clair Avenue (Cleveland), 23, *24,* 26–27, 128
St. Lawrence (Sveti Lovrent; Cleveland), 25–26, 109, 111
St. Vitus (Sveti Vit; Cleveland), 23, 26–27, 109, 111
Saloons, 110
Saussure, Ferdinand de, 5; *Course in General Linguistics,* 6–7; on language as imposing classification, 68; on semiotics of culture, 51, 53, 158 n.3
Secondness. *See* Firstness/Secondness/Thirdness
Semiosphere, 7, 63
Semiotic portraits in cultural context: social change and psychological consequences, 127–29; theoretical fieldwork issues, 130–31. *See also* Human signs in cultural context
Semiotics of culture, 50–73, 157–58 n.1; and abduction, 71, 72; Bakhtin on, 50, 64–66, 153; and boundaries, 50, 59–60, 135–36; and everyday behavior, 50, 60; and folk costumes, 53–54, 131; and gesture, 53; and history/memory, 50, 61–62, 70; history/theories of, 5–8; Jakobson on, 50, 53, 54–55; Lotman's semiosphere concept, 63; Moscow-Tartu School on, 55, 56–63; Mukařovský on, 54; Peirce on, 51–53; and postmodern studies, 50, 67–70; and power, 62, 72–73; Prague School on, 53, 54, 61; Saussure on, 51, 53, 158 n.3; and theory vs. fact, 71–72; Wolf on, 72–73, 153. *See also* Culture texts

Senapur (North Central India), 86
Shattuk, Roger, 69
Singer, Milton B., 54–55, 157–58 n.1
Singh, R. D., 86
Slivnica, Mount, 78, 83, 97–98
Slovene-American choral societies, 41
Slovene Hayrack, The (Čop and Cevc), 59
Slovene Immigrant History, 1900–1950 (I.
   Molek), 118, 121–23, 152
Slovene immigrants, 123. *See also* Cleve-
   land settlement; Hibbing settlement
Slovene language, 19, 77–78, 108, 111
Slovene National Benefit Society (Slov-
   enska Narodna Podporna Jednota;
   Cleveland), 23, 109, 111, 115
Slovene National Home (Slovenski dom;
   Cleveland), 23, 26–27, 110
Slovene National Library (Slovenska
   narodna čitalnica; Cleveland), 26–27
Slovene National Reading Room (Slovenska narodna čitalnica; Cleveland),
   110
Slovene Workmen Association (Cleveland), 24
Slovenia: Austrian rule of, 88–89; Catholicism in, 19; communist/post-
   communist periods, official record in,
   18–19; economy of, 94; emigration
   from, 3–4, 94, 106–7; establishment
   of, 89–90; ethnic makeup of, 19; forest
   land in, 87, *135*; independence for, 9,
   18–19, 90, 94, 152; indigenous tradition vs. ideology/invented tradition
   in, 36–37; poverty in, 87, 88, 129;
   Slovene-American choral societies'
   travel to, 41; traditional values of, 144;
   work ethic in, 148
Slovenska domovina (The Slovene
   Homeland; Cleveland), 23
Slovenski sokol (Slovene Falcon; Cleveland), 110
Smugglers, The (Hace), 87
Smuggling, 87, 90, 131–32
Snežnik, Mount, 78
Social change and psychological conse-
   quences, 127–29
Society, 31–33, 42
Society of Tourist Guides for Notranjsko,
   97

Sokol (Falcon) gymnastics group (Cleve-
   land), 110
Šteberk: castle at, 14, 16; prince of, 81–82
Stoics, 5–6
Strike, The (Eisenstein), 57
Structural vs. astructural, 56
Sušelj, Rudolph (Susel), 111
Suspicion, 68
Symbol, 61, 153. *See also* Icon/Index/
   Symbol

Tambiah, Stanley, 33
Tedlock, Dennis, 64
Telič, Jože, 102
Text, definitions of, 44
Theoretical fieldwork issues, 130–31
Theory vs. fact, 71–72
Thirdness. *See* Firstness/Secondness/
   Thirdness
Tito, Josip Broz, 18, 91, 92
Tolstoy, Leo, 131
Tourism, 20; and memory/history, 49;
   and nostalgia, 154; and tradition, 39;
   in Žerovnica, 20, 49, 72, 92–93, 95–98,
   96, 104–5, 152
Tourist farms, 96, 97
Tradition: after communism's fall, 37; vs.
   custom, 36; and ethnic cleansing, 38;
   and the global village, 37; indigenous
   vs. invented, 35–38; revitalization of,
   38–40, 42; and tourism, 39
Traditional values, 144
Transnational ethnic culture texts, 43
Transnationalism, 3, 32, 35, 43
Triglav Choral and Dramatic Society
   (Cleveland), 110
Triglav Mountain, 110
Tripartite Pact (1941), 90
Turkman, Andrew, 110–11
Turkman, Josephine, 110–11
Turner, Victor, 45–46, 57, 65–66, 158n.2
Two Worlds (I. Molek), 118, 121
Tyler, Stephen A., 69
Tynjanov, Jurij, 53

Unemployment, 94
Uspensky, Boris, 6; on ethnicity, 131; on
   everyday behavior, 50, 60, 154; on historical perception, 61–62; on laughter,
   65–66; on memory/history, 50, 154;

on pre-Christian practices in Russia, 47; on semantic dominant, 153

Valvasor, Johann W., 79, 83, 97
Valvasor Promenade (1993), 97
Van Gennep, Arnold, 45
Vernadsky, V. I., 63
Vico, Giovanni Battista, 5–6
Vilfan, Sergij, 86–87

West vs. East, 40–41
Witches, 83
Wolf, Eric, 69; on the individual, 31–32; on semiotics of culture, 72–73, 153; on society, 31, 154

Yates, Edmund, 48
Yugoslavia: communal administration in, 92; ethnic violence in, 8, 9, 18; formation of, 18, 89–90; German invasion of, 90
Yugoslav Kingdom, 80

Zadruga (cooperative or community), 79, 84, 86–87, 158 n.2
Zarja (Cleveland), 41, 110–11, 114, 115, 117
Zastava (Flag; Cleveland), 111
Zemlja (land measure), 17–18, 157 nn.3–4
Žerovnica (Slovenia), 78–105; and America, impressions of, 95–98; anticommunist sentiment in, 15, 17; autobiographies of villagers, 98–103; Brest furniture factory, 11, 17, 20, 90–91; building in, laws governing, 97; carnival behavior/celebrations in, 66, 87–88, 91–92, *104*; Catholic Church's decline in, 91; Cleveland connections, evidence of, 5; communist/postcommunist periods in, 19–20, 128, 129; conflicts within, nonverbal signs of, 44–45; dispute settlement in, juridical, 91; economy of, 84, 87–91, 93–95, 127, 140–41; 1848 to communist period, 87–90; elders in, support of, 127–29, 152, 153, 154; elite of, 91, 96–97, 104; emigration from, 3, 88; emigrés' visits to, 88, 137, 153; ethnic conflicts' affects on, 20; field work in, 94–95, *95*; history of, 80–87; history preserved by villagers of, 48, 49; houses in, 17–18, 48–49, 80, 92; in-group feeling/work ethic in, 128; internal space of, 59; land distribution/use in, 11, 13, *13*, 14–15, 17–18, 20, 84, 94; location/layout of, 11, *12*, 13–16, 78–80; Marof cooperative farm, 11, 16–17, 79–80, 90–91; method of studying, 25; modernization in, 93, 95, 127, 128–29; 1960s to present, 11–18, *13–15*; nostalgia in, 154; objects as symbols in, 61; origin/social organization of, 84–87; partisan monument, 13, *14*, 15, 61; postcommunist period, 92–103, 154; remittances to, 87, 88–89; sociopolitical inequities in, 15, 17–18, 92–93; Šteberk castle, 14, 16; stores in, private, 95; Sveti Pavel, 13, *15*, 16; tax collector as sign of power in, 73; threshing dramatizations in, 58; tourism in, 20, 49, 72, 92–93, 95–98, *96*, 104–5, 152; traditional arts in, 91–92; traditions as re-emerging in, 39; Turkish invasion of, 80–81; unemployment in, 94; upward mobility of youth in, 152; World War II and communist decades, 90–92. *See also* Cerknica Lake
Zora (Dawn; Cleveland), 110
Zvon (The Bell; Cleveland), 110

Irene Portis-Winner is retired Professor of Anthropology, Massachusetts College of Art, Boston. She is the author of *The Semiotics of Culture: The "Strange Intruder"* (1993) and *A Slovenia Village: Zerovnica* (1971). She is the editor of *Dynamics of East European Ethnicities Outside of Eastern Europe with Special Emphasis on the American Case* (1983; with T. G. Winner), *The Peasant and the City in Eastern Europe: Changing Socio-Economic Levels of Culture* (1984; with J. Umiker-Sebeok), and *Semiotics of Culture* (1979).

Library of Congress Cataloging-in-Publication Data

Portis-Winner, Irene.
Semiotics of peasants in transition : Slovene villagers and their ethnic relatives in America / Irene Portis-Winner.
p. cm. — (Sound and Meaning: The Roman Jakobson series in linguistics and poetics)
Includes bibliograpical references and index.
ISBN 0-8223-2827-5 (cloth : alk. paper) — ISBN 0-8223-2841-0 (pbk. : alk. paper)
1. Ethnicity—Slovenia. 2. Slovene Americans—Ethnic identity. 3. Culture—Semiotic models. I. Title. II. Sound and meaning.
DR1373 .W56 2002
305.8'0094373—dc21   2001007554